PAY OR BURN

**Bible-based Help
To Make Purse-happy
Christians**

BY G. WILLIAM GENSZLER

FAIRWAY PRESS
Lima, Ohio

PAY OR BURN

FIRST EDITION
Copyright © 1992 by
G. William Genszler, D.D.

All rights reserved. No portion of this book may be reproduced or utilized in any form or by any means, electronic or mechanical including photocopying, without permission in writing from the publisher. Inquiries should be addressed to: Fairway Press, 628 South Main Street, Lima, Ohio 45804.

7952 / ISBN 1-55673-529-4   PRINTED IN U.S.A.

Dedication

I would like to dedicate this book to those who have given me revealing insight into the exciting and proper stewardship of wealth . . .

Foremost among them is my Blessed Lord Jesus, who by His Word and example revealed to me the munificence of God's bounty and His never failing Grace. To God be the Glory. Amen.

I would like to thank God for my late father, the Reverend George W. Genszler of Racine, who by word and deed demonstrated a lifestyle that reflects a stewardship that illustrated God's service through His church.

I would also like to add a "thank you" to the Lutheran Laymen's Movement for Stewardship that was organized in the days of the old United Lutheran Church. Many years ago this group of dedicated men saw that the church was suffering great financial hardship because of the lack of support. This was due in part to the ignorance of the response its members should have had to the stewardship of time, talent and money. These brave men each contributed a minimum of $100 a year to underwrite programs of Christian Stewardship as a lifestyle. Under the slogan "Stewardship is the practice of the Christian religion" coined by the late Dr. Greever, this group became a real catalyst to lead the whole church to a greater understanding of the real joys of "Graceful Giving." For years this group provided congregations with tracts, articles, pledge cards, etc., free of charge. Today they have changed their name to Lutheran Laity Movement to include women among their active members. This group of dedicated lay people feel called of God to bear fruit for His Kingdom in a very special way, bringing glory to His Holy Name. May their tribe increase.

Acknowledgement

Since this book is concerned with Faithfulness, I feel compelled to acknowledge that I have discovered a few minor mistakes concerning dates and locations. I am sure you can understand how easily this can happen, especially when you have 50 years of memory to contend with. These mistakes in minor details should not in any way destroy the events of the story I relate. Memory has a way of playing tricks on everyone of us. It is my sincere hope and prayer that this little volume will help you be aware that all Stewardship is God's activity in the church through us. Thus, all of our giving our time, talent and treasure is GRACE giving and falls under the category of Worship.

Table Of Contents

The Main Purpose Of This Book	7
Chapter 1	
Pay Or Burn	9
Chapter 2	
Faith Or Formula	15
Chapter 3	
Rais'n Or Prais'n	21
Chapter 4	
Reasonable Act Of Worship	27
Chapter 5	
Hedge Or Pledge	33
Chapter 6	
Tithing At Its Best	39
Chapter 7	
Stewardship Sermon In Four Parts	43
Chapter 8	
How Are You Going To Manage?	59
Chapter 9	
A Dimes Worth Of Trust	67
Chapter 10	
Beyond Gratitude	75
Chapter 11	
The Chance Of A Lifetime	81
Chapter 12	
Stewardship Ideas	93
Chapter 13	
Show And Tell	107
Chapter 14	
Appeals Not Appalling	111
Chapter 15	
Fund Raisers	115
Chapter 16	
Com"Mission" Or Volunteer	119
Chapter 17	
Dis-Interested	123

Chapter 18
    Risky Business 125
Chapter 19
    Ecumenism-Opportunity Unlimited 129
        In Conclusion 133

The Main Purpose Of This Book

All my life I have been vitally interested in Stewardship in the Church because it is really **God's activity** in my life and the life of the Church. Unfortunately, many people miss this important aspect of Stewardship and consequently they make many foolish mistakes in their approach to this joyful experience.

We often forget that when you are saved by God's Grace, even your faith and your stewardship are all His doing. Recall how St. Paul said, "It is not I, but Christ that worketh within me."

It brings to mind a story I heard in my first parish in the Badlands of North Dakota.

Legend had it that when the local hotel caught fire, the new volunteers rushed to the rescue. When the Chief arrived at the scene, he found some of his beginners busy at work trying to save what they could. Unfortunately, they got their priorities all mixed up and were throwing all the crockery, wash basins and pitchers out the window while others were carrying the mattresses down the steps.

It has disturbed me that so many pastors and congregations make such a mess out of their stewardship approach to their people. They literally throw out the very essential things that make stewardship truly Christian and substitute a lot of manmade gimmicks to try to improve the stewardship of their people, especially in the area of money.

Thanks be to God there is a better way and since stewardship involves sharing, I must share what I have learned about God's service in the church through us.

Pastor G. William Genszler

CHAPTER 1
Pay Or Burn

Pay Day

I shall never forget the day I stopped in at the Dells Grill for a spot of coffee and was delighted to be joined by a young Episcopal Priest fresh out of seminary. Word had come from his Bishop to preach to his people concerning their giving to the church. Frankly, he was uneasy about talking about money. We chatted for a while and then he rose to go back to his office to work on his sermon. As he left me he jokingly said, "Wish me luck, Bill. I've got to go and write one of those blasted PAY OR BURN sermons . . ."

After he left I got to thinking about his phrase PAY OR BURN. It then dawned on me that there are a lot of pastors and lay people who have this concept about money in the church. Face it. It is a touchy subject matter; but why? I believe I have part of the answer and it all boils down to the fact that the stewardship of wealth has been **wrongly taught** and **wrongly practices** in the Church. In a way, I believe that the Church itself has been one of the greatest offenders forever sending the wrong message to its people about giving, especially giving of money.

It happened in Jesus' day. The rulers of the temple failed to heed God's word concerning the methods He wanted them to use to finance His kingdom through graceful giving and thankful tithing. Instead they concocted a new gimmick for raising extra funds by selling their special doves at a profit and then charging exorbitant rates of exchange. It was another case of PAY OR BURN. If you wanted the blessings of the Temple, you had to pay through the nose to get it. No wonder Jesus was vehement and drove the money changers out. They had made God's house of prayer for all people into a den of thieves and a house of merchandise.

It happened again in Luther's day when the Church at Rome wanted to increase its income to finance the building of St. Peter's Cathedral. This time the gimmick was the selling of Indulgences. Tetzel came offering release of a soul from purgatory as soon as the money hit the bottom of the box. It was another case of PAY OR BURN. Fortunately God sent Martin Luther to upset the carts of the money racketeers to proclaim anew that God's Grace is a gift and it can't be bought or sold. He announced that God has done everything necessary for our salvation and because God has done it all, there is just everything for us to do in grateful response to, "Thank, Praise, Serve, and Obey Him."

In the light of such wondrous Grace and Love — the phrase PAY OR BURN can take on new meaning.

BURN . . . no longer the Flames of Hell fanned by guilt and fear but Burn like the flames of the Holy Spirit that settles over the heads of the disciples on the Day of Pentecost. Aflame with the Spirit they weren't just better people but they had become new creatures in Christ. Burn . . . symbolized the new spirit of Joy and thankfulness that flooded their hearts. Again, when I thought of BURN I thought of the event in the life of the two disciples on the road to Emmaus. Recall how they mentioned that "their hearts burned within them" as they experieneced the living presence of the resurrected Lord.

PAY . . . The longer I live and the more the Lord makes Himself known to me through Word and Sacrament, the more I am convinced that the only true motive for stewardship that is authentic is found in Christ, who through the Holy Spirit can set our hearts aflame with His wondrous Grace. When a person is aflame with God's redeeming Grace then that person is ready to PAY everything in thanksgiving. Recall St.

Paul's words, "with our eyes wide open to the mercies of God we just want to give our very body as a living sacrifice (not in order to win brownie points with God) but as a reasonable act of worship."

Isn't that the point our offertory prayer tries to make which reads, "Merciful Father, we offer with joy and thanksgiving what you have first given us — ourselves, our time, and our possessions, signs of your gracious love. Receive them for the sake of Him who offered Himself for us, Jesus Christ, our Lord. Amen."

Please God

This then is the Spirit that should dominate and motivate all of our Stewardship in the Church and especially the stewardship of MONEY, SO THAT WHAT WE OFFER TO GOD IS PLEASING IN HIS SIGHT. I am sure that God must wince at some of the gimmicks many churches use to try to raise funds, never realizing what irreparable harm they are doing to their members by sending them the whole wrong message about stewardship of wealth. Oh, I admit many times they do raise sums of money but at what cost? I think it was T. S. Elliot who said, "There was no greater treason than to do the right thing for the wrong reason."

St. Paul spotted the danger in wrongful giving and that is why he emphatically wrote, "let everyone give as their heart tells them, not grudgingly or under compulsion for it is a known fact that God loves a cheerful giver, those whose heart is in their gift." Christ verifies this truth by the way he excitedly highlighted the widow's giving as most acceptable to God and again the "beautiful giving" of Mary of Bethany as she poured out her devotion and thanks through the precious ointment.

Fragrance Or Stench

Recall the words of Paul to the Church at Phillipi, " Your generosity, is like a lovely fragrance, a sacrifice that pleases the very heart of God." Great — that changes the nature and character of giving from guilt ridden chore to blessed privilege. The attitude of gratitude changes giving from being a collection into an offering, from burdensome duty to joyful worship. In light of this insight to the true meaning of the stewardship of wealth, I have always made it a practice to inform my congregations, "look, if you can't give your money out of a loving heart, keep it for it will damn you more that it will bless you." Remember Cain's offering, given in a sour spirit. It never got off the ground, but only proves to fuel his hatred for both God and his brother.

What Gives

Long ago the Psalmist asked the question, "What shall I render unto my God for all of His benefits to me?" He came to the conclusion that the only decent response that would be worthy of God's overwhelming Grace would be set forth in the following actions. "I will render the sacrifices of thanksgiving." That means more than a swimming feeling of gratitude. Recall how David once stated that he would never offer to God that which cost him nothing. The Psalmist lists some of the things he would do to get beyond gratitude to the actual giving of thanks. First, he would go to church. "I will enter His courts with praise. I will pay my vow before the whole congregation. I will bring an offering." Just why would he do all this? Was it guilt or his attempt to escape the fires of hell? Not by a long shot. It was because God through the Holy Spirit had set his heart aflame with His steadfast love and grace.

Grace Giving

I still remember to this day the little offertory hymn we sang in Sunday school that never let us forget the only true motive for our returning to God our gifts of love. The song ran:

> *"Saviour, thy dying love, thou gavest me*
> *Nor should I ought withold, Dear Lord from Thee.*
> *In love my soul would bow, my heart fulfill its vow*
> *Some offering bring Thee now, something for Thee."*

It is as simple as that. Giving will become a joyful experience because it is motivated by Love. Without Love (AGAPE) even our giving can become a drag and a waste of effort. Recall how St. Paul stated it in the 13th Chapter of 1 Corinthians: *"Even though I sell all that I have and give it to the poor, if I have not love it is nothing."*

On the other hand, when I let Christ become the object of my affection, then I discover to my everlasting joy that "nothing I ever do for Him is ever lost or wasted (Phillips translation of I Corinthians 15:58)." When a pastor becomes aware of the joyful privilege we have in giving and sharing — that pastor will never again say, "I have to write one of those blasted PAY OR BURN sermons again."

CHAPTER 2
Faith Or Formula

Giving . . . An Art Not A Science

All too often we in the church turn the matter of increased giving into a science with special formulas for extracting extra money from the members of the congregation. There are dozens of plans on the market that are guaranteed to get you more money, but unfortunately that is all they will do. Many times the emphasis of some of these campaigns do more harm than good, because they only force the council to look around for another gimmick to use next year. A stewardship program that is built on "fast buck programs" is self defeating. It reminds me of a faith that is built on miracles. It always has to have even greater miracles in order to maintain itself. Christ himself warned us about those whose faith is built on miracles and not on Him. He said it was an evil and adulterous generation that was always looking for signs and wonders. Truly, it must sadden the heart of our Lord to see to what shallow depths His church will stoop in order to raise funds. The tragedy of it all is that it is so unnecessary to have to go through all of these manipulations in order to finance the spiritual programs of both the local congregations and the Church at large.

Lord, Teach Us How To Give

It became increasingly evident to the disciples, that even though they prayed, nothing very exciting came out of it all.

Like so many people today, they had the idea that "prayer changes things," when in reality "prayer releases God's power," which changes people and their willingness to learn to do the will of their Heavenly Father. Out of necessity, the disciples asked Jesus, "Lord teach us how to pray." His very answer to their request was to lift their heart and eyes to a new art form and began with the wonder and the beauty of a Heavenly Father whose very Name was Holy and whose abode was Heaven. He pictured the wonder of God's kingdom where the joyous will of heaven reigns supreme and offered us a taste of the same. When His will is done on Earth with the same glorious abandon as it is done so perfectly in heaven.

What can be said of prayer holds true in the area of giving. When you think of it, "giving that is pleasing to God" is in itself a distinct form of prayer. It comes under the heading of "worship." The scriptures abound with expressions of praise to God coupled with gifts and sacrifices to express love and gratitude to the Lord. This kind of giving enhances our joy. Recall the words of scripture (2 Corinthians 9:7-15, Phillip translation) where it said, *"God loves the person whose heart is in their gift."*

This kind of joyful giving is available to all members in our congregation, but unfortunately many of our people never get the chance to practice this art.

Begin At The Beginning

In my many years in the ministry I have found that too many churches never instruct their new members in the Art of Giving. I always made it a practice to make it quite clear where our congregation stood with regards to the Stewardship of Wealth and what was expected of all of its members. Below is a copy of a letter I would give our prospective members in which the program was spelled out and I would take the time to go through the following letter with the new members:

The Grace Of Giving

Many people make a botch out of their giving to the Church because they never have known the real reason for "Why we give" and "How we give" so that it is acceptable to God.

St. Paul says that people who give grudgingly and out of necessity find no blessing. Remember Cain in Genesis. His whole attitude about his offering to God destroyed both his relationship to God and his brother. As Christians, we are to be good stewards of all of God's gifts to us. My definition of Stewardship is as follows: *Stewardship receives the whole of life as a gracious Gift of God and uses all of it so everyone is aware of its source.*

Six things to consider:

1. We ask our members not to give primarily "*to* something" such as budgets, special needs etc.

2. We do ask our members to give primarily "*from* something" — from a grateful heart to God for all of His grace.

3. We ask our members never to think of their giving to the church as "charity." God doesn't need charity: He seeks our love.

4. Our church never publishes lists of names concerning how much or how little each member gives.

5. We never try to "raise money for the church" through suppers, sales (merchandising).

6. We have no fees, no dues. We don't pay to the church or give to the church . . . WE DO ASK OUR MEMBERS TO SUPPORT THE CHURCH BECAUSE WE LOVE HER LORD.

(All giving in this Church must be based upon the free-will of each individual. It must come as an act of worship and thanksgiving to God for His blessings to us. No other reason will do.)

Because our giving springs out of grateful hearts to God, it will be proportionate giving. "To whom much is given, from him much is required." God never asks us for that which He Himself does not first provide.

The question need never arise, "How much shall I give?" The real question, for every member to ask is, "How much do I love my Lord and how grateful am I for all His benefits to me?" You see — giving is an *act of worship*. I will put my wealth into those things that I feel have real and lasting WORTH. That is what the word WORSHIP means. It comes from the words — WORTH-SHIP."

We are not left in the dark as to how and what we should give — not since we have God's Word to guide us in the reasonable stewardship of our wealth.

St. Paul instructed the early church members —

"Let a man set aside on the first day of the week according to the way the Lord has prospered him."

TO SET ASIDE — means *planned* giving. Love never throws in its leftovers. It sets its gifts aside first. Pledging a definite amount for each week's gift is a convenient way for me to keep God foremost in my sense of real values. It is a testimony to my own heart that I am confident that God does provide all things, even my ability to pledge. It is an act of Faith!

We expect every member to make a weekly pledge of support. A pledge is not a rigid legal promissory note. It is an expression of my intention to do so much regularly (as St. Paul suggests — on the first day of each week). Naturally, a pledge can be changed — either raised or lowered — by the simple means of a note or a call to our church treasurer in the eventuality of sickness or a change in income. That is what Paul means by "as a man prospers." This is proportionate giving.

What Proportion Should I Give?

Again, God's word suggests that the TITHE BELONGS TO THE LORD. This means that He has commanded that the very first 10 percent of all that I receive belongs to Him and that I have no right to use it for myself. It was His way of reminding all of us — that all we have comes from Him as a loan to us as good stewards of His grace. More and more of our people in this congregation have found the promise of God thrillingly true concerning that which He said about the TITHE. *"Try me,"* says the Lord, *"and see if I will not open the windows of heaven and pour down on you such a blessing that you will not be able to receive it all."*

Our suggestion to all new members is simply this: *Why not set your goal on the tithe?* Begin today to move in that direction. Begin by setting a definite percentage of your income aside (you set the percentage, 3 percent, 5 percent, 8 percent, 10 percent) *or whatever your heart tells you*. Then plan to grow each year in the grace of Christian giving. GRATITUDE THAT GROWS is evidence that our FAITH IS ROOTED IN CHRIST.

How Shall I Divide My Pledge?

Our church has two funds that we all try to support to the best of our ability. They are the CURRENT FUND; this is for the operation of the program in our Church. It pays salaries, heats the building, etc. The BENEVOLENCE FUND; this is the heart of Chrisitan Outreach through Missions and mercy. BOTH FUNDS ARE IMPORTANT AND DESERVE OUR LOVING SUPPORT. Our synod has suggested that we consider at least 65 percent for Current Fund and 35 percent for Benevolence. Some of us make it 50/50. Do what your heart suggests.

Learn early from your Lord to be a Gracious Giver.

Prayer

Lord, give me Grace to grow.
not just in years or time,

Age marks not the progress of the soul
TIME only shows a space to grow
upward in thy love divine
Lord, let me grow.

Lord, let my SOUL grow,
let it mature in gratitude
and render thanks with more than lip or hand
Let me grow outward in thy plan
to show thy love to fellowman
Lord, let me grow. Amen.

G. Wm. Genszler (1955)
"Grow in Grace"

CHAPTER 3
Rais'n Or Prais'n

Church "Chicken-Catch-Or-Glory?"

Some churches are known by their official name in the community but other churches are recognized by their commercial activities. I recall a town that had two churches. One was called the Church of the Heavenly Chicken Supper and the other was known for its Lutefisk Suppers. Some churches have Elegant Bazaars and others shout "Bingo" louder than "Hallelujah."

I was always grateful to God that when I served my first parish, our National Church had made it a practice to cut out all commercialism in the name of the church. This stance didn't come easy because a good many churches in the East supported their work with Chicken Corn Soup Suppers and fancy fairs to raise money. The United Lutheran Church in 1930 made it a policy that they would not support any mission congregation that indulged in commercialism. All of the support for the new churches was to come about through an Every Member Visitation where each family was invited to pledge their support for the coming year. All of this seemed to be a very sensible plan and it did take up some of the slack in meeting the budget for the coming year.

I remember the Fall of 1940 when I became the pastor of St. John's Lutheran Church in Killdeer, North Dakota. I was informed by the Board of American Missions that all of the pledges of support for the coming year had to be sent into the

Board before I would receive our Mission Board Salary support. I discovered that in the past the pastor was pretty much responsible for gathering up such pledges as he could. Of course it meant calling at every home and ranch. Some of those ranches were 45 miles from the church down in Badlands. I didn't mind this task because it gave me an opportunity to meet the people in their homes and thus we became acquainted. One thing I did learn was how destitute these people were. They had suffered drought, grasshoppers and hail, year after year, for twelve years, but they had an unbeatable spirit.

My visit always meant staying for a meal and it was after the meal that they would say, "Well pastor, I suppose you would like to have our check for the support of the church for the coming year." On a whole, this usually amounted to about ten dollars. Naturally I thanked them for their support. But in the conversation following I would mention to them that we had a widow in the congregation with five children who annually made her pledge to the church and paid it every Sunday. The pledge was for fifty cents a Sunday, didn't sound like much, but by the end of the year she had contributed $26.00.

I am sure that they all knew who this widow was and I am sure they could easily figure out that she was giving almost three times what they were giving. The widow's mite was a mighty good promoter to help others get a vision of the joy of sacrificial giving.

Frozen Assets Thaw

It was in my second year at this same parish when it became time for another Every Member Visit because the pledges had to be in the New York office before we would receive salary aid. Then something happened. We got hit with a good old fashioned North Dakota blizzard with twenty-two foot drifts. What do you do in a case like that? Simple, PRAY GOD AND TELL THE PEOPLE . . . And that is exactly what I did. The

Lord answered my prayer with a great idea (a new idea back then). Why not encourage all of our people to attend church and as an act of worship make their prayerful commitment to God in God's House with no pressure or duress placed on anyone other than their love of Christ. I set about writing a letter to each family explaining our situation. I appealed to them as loyal followers of Christ to plan to attend services the first Sunday of Advent and as an act of worship joyfully and faithfully make their commitment to support the church because of their love for Him who is Lord of the Church.

Heat Wave

Much to my joy, the Lord gave us a harvest that we just couldn't believe. People came to church, they received the pledges of Salvation in the Lord's Supper and they in return opened their hearts and joyfully pledged their overwhelming support for the coming year. Many in the congregation admitted that for the first time in their life, they felt the warm sense of "blessedness" that comes from generous giving to the Lord. Many of them said, "Let's do this again next year." I began to see just what was happening. THE RIGHT MESSAGE WAS GETTING THROUGH TO GOD'S PEOPLE. Giving was no longer a chore, a distasteful necessity. There was no pressure of neighbor embarrassing neighbor by "putting the bite on them." In the past, pledging on the Every Member Visitation was more like giving to charity, like the United Way, or Easter Seals, etc. That is fine for those organizations, but somehow giving to the church must be different. It must never be classified as a "charity drive." GOD DOESN'T NEED MY CHARITY! The reverse is true. It is I who live by His Grace and His Charity. I am convinced that the church should never beg. God is no Beggar standing at the end of the line with a tin cup looking for leftovers.

The Great Discovery

Even I felt the exhilaration of this whole new approach to Graceful Giving to the Lord's work. The more I studied the scriptures, the more I became aware that this promotes the kind of giving that the Lord loves. "The Lord loves a cheerful giver — a giver whose heart is in their gift." We sent in the list of pledges we received from our first Loyalty Sunday. The Director of the Board of American Missions couldn't believe that our giving had increased from an average of $11 per family to $85 per family per year. That year our little congregation rose to 11th place in per capita giving for Benevolence. We remodeled the church, purchased a parsonage, and paid off a twenty-year-old mortgage. But most important was the rich treasure of Faith placed in our hearts as we proved the reality of faith and trust in God's amazing grace.

As I watched the reaction in our congregation I was reminded of that incredible scene in 2 Chronicles 29:27 which states, "And when the burnt offering began then began the song of the Lord with trumpets!"

Great Day In The Morning

In my forty-two years in the active ministry serving both small mission congregations as well as very large congregations with more than 2,500 members, I firmly believe that there is no method or program that can begin to match the spiritual growth and impact of a well-planned and joyfully executed Loyalty Sunday approach.

The key to the success of such a program is the long range preparation that goes into making this an annual festival event. There are no tricks, no gimmicks, no snappy sleight of hand to try to pry a few extra dollars out of members of the congregation. People are not dumb. They soon become wary of such tactics and they build up a whole set of defensive moves to protect their pocket books from any and all intruders. The tragedy that ensues is the fact that our people are denied the blessing that is their's from pouring forth their devotion to God for all of His benefits to them. In the next Chapter I will share some things that I have found to be helpful in setting the right tone and motivation for a thrilling Loyalty Sunday.

CHAPTER 4
Reasonable Act Of Worship

Frozen Stewardship

There is an old legend they used to tell in Killdeer, North Dakota, where I had my first parish. They had a very old wooden hotel in the center of town. One day after a winter blizzard hit the town and the temperature dropped to below 30 degrees, a rancher came to town with his team and wagon to pick up supplies. As was his custom, he would drop off at the hotel and try to thaw out his frozen beard. While he was standing close to the pot belly stove, a traveling salesman came down from the second floor and seeing the ice covered rancher exclaimed, "My gosh man, what room did you have?"

Thawed

I have discovered that so many stewardship programs are never quite "thawed" out. The reason being that too often we think of stewardship as a fast shot in the arm that is supposed to miraculously produce great results. Sometimes it works for a year or two, then we have to look around for another gimmick to stir up the troops. There's a lot better way and that way is a Loyalty Sunday Response. Some churches have tried it and haven't been successful. I think I know why. They don't train their people and they don't prepare for it on a year round approach. In Chapter two of this book you will find listed the preparations that are given to all new members entering the congregation. They know exactly where we stand with regards to the support that is expected of those that love the Lord. It is surprising to discover that it is the new members who are the most willing to tithe or move in the direction of tithing. All of our members are continually made aware of the privilege we have of sharing our blessings not only with our own congregation but in the mission support of the whole church. I learned very early in life from my pastor father to stress giving to others. I don't ever think I preached a sermon stressing the giving to the budget or local operational expenses. Benevolence giving, fifty-fifty giving has always been the theme of my stewardship sermons. I learned early that when the benevolence of a church is raised, the current fund automatically goes right along with it. I have always been thrilled to see the congregations I have been privileged to serve rise to the top of the list in the support of the outreach program of the whole church. What is more is I have learned that a pastor should teach the people to be generous by his or her example. I was thrilled by the response of a congregation that I served for 28 years when they were approached for sizable amounts of money for the college and for the seminary. When they learned what the per capita goal was, they tripled it and paid it in full without having a campaign to accomplish it. It can be done. It is the result of simply *"Pray God and tell the people."*

Don't Fence Me In

All year long we make it a point to keep our people informed as to the exciting things they are doing through their gifts. I have discovered some pastors try to hide and protect their members from the outreach causes of the church because they foolishly have a feeling that it might cut into their local budgets. I guess that is one of the reasons I am not fond of a "unified budget" where the church board determines how much of the income will be designated for Benevolence giving. I have noticed that churches that adopt such a program usually have a big drop in benevolence giving. Foolishly they don't understand that benevolent giving is the motivating factor that helps people become more generous. I know of a church that was giving close to $80,000 a year to Benevolence and is now only giving $40,000 a year because they went to the unified budget. A layman said, "I cannot understand my pastor who preaches, 'Give and it will be given unto you,' yet has given us just the reverse attitude when he called for a unified budget." I know several people who have actually cut their pledge to their local congregation because they don't want any church, pastor, or council dictating to them to give less to benevolence. Never limit your people and their giving by selfish tactics to keep more money at home. Teach your people to care, to care enough to give the very best. They will respond with gusto and their generosity will reflect at home as well. Jesus wasn't kidding when He reminded us "Give and it will be given unto you, pressed down, shaken together and running over." Believe me, it works not because it is a clever gimmick but because it is rooted in the spirit of our Lord and His Word. Trust Him. I think raising the giving pattern of a congregation is a breeze when you realize that this is God's people and He has ways through the working of the Holy Spirit to set hearts aflame with generous love. Again, it is *"Pray God and Tell the people"* and then get out of the way and share the fun with your people to become agents of His Glory.

When Is The Best Time?

I have always felt that the Stewardship Program does not do well when it is done in October or November. There are just too many interruptions. Duck hunting, deer hunting, football and people going to close up cottages. Another thing, there seems to be a bit of anxiety among people at this time of the year. This is also the dregs, the end of the church year. I prefer

Advent. The season of the church year that means new beginning. A time to wake up to reality. A time for repentance and renewal. A period when the thrill of the birth of the Christ Child is near. A period when people are thinking about giving gifts. A time when church attendance begins to swell. A time when there is a renewed sense of worship in the air. *"O Come, let us adore Him"* and *"They came bearing gifts."* Can't you begin to catch the logic of this kind of thinking? Sometimes we set the first Sunday of Advent as Loyalty Communion Sunday, and the Second Sunday in Advent as Loyalty Commitment Sunday. When your people are trained over the years, you will find that 65 to 70 percent will come to church and here, as an act of worship, make their pledge for the coming year. There is no pressure upon them other than the Word of God and believe me, you don't have to look very far in the Bible to find plenty of ammunition to speak to them lovingly about God and Money and their support and their love. It works because it matches his example, "For God so loved the World, He gave His only begotten Son."

Loyalty Sunday Follow Up

On Monday morning the office sends out a letter to those who didn't make it. We tell them about the wonderful day we had and how sorry we were that they were forced to miss the fun, but because we want them to share the joy, they will be given an opportunity this coming Sunday immediately following the services. Here we ask them to remain and meet with the Chairman of the Stewardship Committee and then they can make their pledge. However, if they would rather have someone come to their home to receive their peldge, visitation teams will be happy to oblige on the next Sunday afternoon. Usually we get between 15 to 20 percent more pledges on the following Sunday. Once people get in the habit of coming to church to make their commitment they seem to do it in a joyful spirit.

*Helpful Hint:

I always make it a practice to have a hymn before the Sermon on Loyalty Sunday and it is during the hymn that ushers pass out the pledge cards. We ask the congregation to receive the card and wait until the end of the sermon when they will be given an opportunity to fill in their pledge. They are then instructed to place their pledge in the basket in the center aisle as they come to communion.

CHAPTER 5
Hedge Or Pledge

No "Ands, Ifs, Or Butts"

Jesus said, "and they with one accord began to make excuse." I'm sure that you recognized these words as part of the parable concerning the response of many who were invited to the Wedding Feast.

I recall a very humorous story told by another pastor at a banquet concerning this very issue. There was a very young self-taught minister, low on education but full of fire and brimstone. When he came to that part of the parable concerning the various excuses given, he became very dramatic and said something like this.

"And the first man invited said, 'Look, I would love to come to the wedding BUT . . . I just bought a parcel of land and I must go and check it out' . . . and the second man said, 'I would love to come BUT I bought a yoke of oxen, pray have me excused," and the third man responded in much the same fashion saying, 'I would love to come BUT I married a wife.' " It was at this point that the pastor exploded and cried, "That is the trouble with the world. There are just too many people trying to slide into heaven on their BUTTS."

Something Inexcusable

I must admit one of the most difficult parts of the ministry is listening to all the weak insipid excuses and alibis that people will give for not participating in the greater work of the Kingdom of God. I have found it particularly true when it comes to the question of the giving of money. Years ago all these excuses were called "pocketbook protection." One day I sat down and decided to "count the ways" that people will try to avoid facing up to their responsibility and stewardship of wealth. It all came to me in poetic form which I have titled "Grace or Disgrace." Let me share it with you.

Grace Or Disgrace

Some people will bluff and set forth the view
    "The Lord's Grace is free so nothing is due,"
       . . . but I'd be ashamed.
Some say that it's wrong to give 'til it hurts
    So they give very little in occasional spurts,
       . . . but I'd be ashamed.
Some will give nothing yet loudly they cry
    "The Church is expensive, the demands are too high,"
       . . . but I'd be ashamed.
Some say they will give but won't bother to pledge
    Their intentions are showing, they're planning to hedge,
       . . . but I'd be ashamed.
Some say they love Jesus, they're full of such jokes
    Two-bits for the Kingdom, yet twelve fifty for smokes,
       . . . but I'd be ashamed.
Some risk a great deal on their lottery game
    and never support Christ's glorious name,
       . . . but I'd be ashamed.
Yes, I'd be ashamed to insult my dear Lord
    with the dregs from the surplus He has laid at my door,
       . . . lest HE be ashamed.
A tenth I would give of all I possess
    His great love constrains me, I couldn't give less,
       . . . lest we both be ashamed.

I pray Thee Dear Father, please help me to see
   In all of my giving I must be like Thee,
      . . . THEN NONE SHALL BE ASHAMED.

"For God so loved the world that He gave His only begotten Son"

Blow Up

    PBS has some excellent shows produced in England. One of my very favorite comedians is Dave Allen, an Irish Roman Catholic who has some of the funniest jokes I've ever heard. One of the best is a joke about the day the Pope had a heart attack. The cardiologists all gather and they came to the conclusion that the only way they could save the Pope's life was to perform a heart transplant. The call went out all over Italy that the Pope needed a new heart. Was there anyone who would sacrifice their heart so the Pope could live?

    Much to the surprise of everyone, 100,000 people showed up in the piazza of St. Peter's Cathedral. The papal envoy went out on the balcony and told the crowd about the condition of the Pope and that only a heart transplant could save him. The question was, who would be willing to give up their heart so that His Holiness could live? Almost in unison 100,000 hands were raised to the sky. The papal envoy didn't know what to do. Who should he choose for this singular honor? After consultation with other cardinals, they came up with a plan. The papal envoy announced that since they didn't know who to choose, they would leave it up to God. He produced a white feather which he said he would release from the balcony onto the crowd below and whom ever the feather fell on, that person would give their heart for the life of the Pope. The feather was released into the air, caught in the wind, it floated back and forth as it descended on the crowd. When the Papal envoy looked down he saw 100,000 Romans Catholics with lifted faces blowing air through their pursed lips (you might wish to act this out), whoosh, whoosh, whoosh, in an effort to keep the feather aloft.

I know a great many Lutherans, Methodists, etc. whose commitment isn't any better when it comes to making a commitment to the Lord. They affirm, "Of course I love the Lord, but don't ask me to pledge." I wonder who they think they are kidding. I wrote a Pastor's Column on this very topic, let me share it with you.

Pastor's Column

Pledging

I have often heard people say, "I don't believe in pledging. You want to know something, neither do I. I DON'T pledge because I believe in PLEDGING, but I PLEDGE because I believe in GOD. That makes a world of difference. A PLEDGE is an indication that I know in my heart that I do love God and I do trust Him above all things. To me that is first and foremost.

Why Pledge?

That is a good question. Many people pledge to let the Church Council know how much money they can count on to pay all of the bills. This may make sense to some, but I DON'T PLEDGE to satisfy the curiosity of the Church Council.

Then, Why Do I Pledge?

First, I pledge primarily in grateful response to a gracious God who PLEDGED to give His life for me and paid that pledge in full on Calvary.

Second, I pledge because I need to pledge. It is the only way that I can be a thoughtful and generous giver. I want my giving to be more than a flash in a pan, a whim of chance dependent on the variations of my many moods. I don't want my gift to God to simply be leftovers. I relish the joy he promised me in being a cheerful giver.

Third, when I fail to pledge, then I only give when I attend church or when I happen to think about it. Often I will give as I please and what is worse, I only give when I am pleased . . . What a lousy way to run a love affair with the bride of Christ, His Church. No marriage can remain a haven of joy if one of the partners refuses to make a commitment. My pledge to His Church is an indication that we are in this thing together through thick and thin, Sunday after Sunday.

A Pledge Says "I Do"

Pledging isn't everything, but it is the best thing I know of to get a love affair started in the right direction.

CHAPTER 6
Tithing At Its Best

Humor That Helps

It has often been stated that Jesus had a rich sense of humor and He used it again and again in His parables for He knew that humor can open up closed minds and make it possible for great truth to be driven home. I have found that when you talk to people about money and their giving it is often very helpful to use bits of humor. A case in point:

There appeared an ad in the newspaper offering to sell a mint condition Mercedes Benz for $200. The price was so low that most people didn't bother to inquire. They felt that it was joke or a con job. There was one man who thought he had better look it over. When he rang the doorbell, a woman came to the door. He immediately inquired about the auto. Was it a genuine offer? What was wrong with the car, was it "hot," had it been in wreck? The woman assured him that it was a perfectly legitimate offer and that the car was in A-1 shape. She even offered to let him drive the car and see for himself. Well, he was greatly impressed with the quality of the auto so he decided to buy it. After he had made the transaction he said to the woman, "Madam, now that I own the car, please level with me. Why did you sell this car to me at that ridiculous figure?" The woman explained to him the reason. "You see," she said, "the car is not mine. It belongs to my husband who ran away with his secretary and they are living together in Florida. Last week he wired me and asked me to sell his car and send him the money."

Cheerful Giving

I have always liked that little story and used it to demonstrate the fact that a person finds it very easy to be a generous and cheerful giver when you are giving away someone else's money. I remind people that tithing falls under that same kind of category. To be a tither you recognized that all you have belongs to God and He has entrusted it in to your hands to manage and He reminds us that the very first tenth, the tithe, belongs to Him. Since it really isn't mine, I just have a ball in giving it away. A tither never has to worry how much or how little, but how do I divide it among those efforts that are God approved. Really, it's fun to be a tither.

Seriously Now . . .

So many people have twisted the idea of tithing into almost a legalistic rite that they spoil the fun of it. They see it as a duty rather than an expression of grace. Many years ago Dr. Clarence Stoughton, the President of Wittenburg University and head of the Lutheran Laymen's Movement for Stewardship wrote the following article that appeared in pamphlet form. I would like to share it with you:

Two Kinds

He could recognize only two tunes, Mark Twain liked to insist; one was "America" and the other wasn't.

Tithing is much like that too. There are two kinds of tithing. One kind is Christian. The other isn't.

Christian Tithing

Christian tithing begins with Christ. Its whole emphasis is upon Him. The central fact in the life of the Christian is the coming of Jesus Christ into the world to give Himself upon the cross for man. Through Him man comes to God; through Him man finds forgiveness and reconciliation. Here is giving and love that is beyond human understanding. It is grace, God's love given freely without our having deserved or merited any part of it.

And right there is where Christian tithing begins — in man's understanding of that central fact of Christian faith, and in his response to it. For, he asks himself, if God has been so good to me, how can I help but show my thanks to Him in every act of life? And in my giving, how can I do less for His work than set aside at least one-tenth of my income — as a first step? Christian tithing begins with Christ!

The Other Kind

The other kind of tithing begins with Old Testament laws and usually stops there. It is the fact that it stops at that point that compels many Christians to reject tithing. For all too often the tither comes to feel that he has now obeyed God's law and therefore has fulfilled his total obligation as a Christian. And, of course, he hasn't. One never fulfills his obligation to God. He can't. All he can do is to pour forth his gratitude every way possible for God's abundant love. The tithe is one way of saying thanks to God — only one way — a reasonable way.

It Makes A Difference

It makes a difference, you see. The tithe is given, not to win God's favor, nor because I expect Him to return three-tenths next week, nor for any of the other foolish, unChristian reasons that one hears occasionally. Like Zaccahaeus, I have looked into the face of Jesus, and I can no longer say my thanks with trifles. The first of my possessions must go to Him now. At least one-tenth now! Certainly more as soon as I can. For Him. For His love.

The simplest definition, therefore, of Christian tithing is that it is a Christian man tithing. This is not just a play on words. For the point that such a definition emphasizes is that it is not tithing that makes a person Christian. He is a Christian first — through faith in Christ Jesus — and then a tither. Let no one believe that tithing and the tithe are tests of one's Christianity. They are but evidence of one's faith.

Only A Difference

It is all of us that God wants, all of our life. The tithe, therefore, is never the final expression of our love. It's only a beginning. Some, in their abundance, undoubtedly can and must go far beyond the tithe. But for most of us it is the least we can do in our gratitude to Him for all His goodness to us.

Forever Our Thanks

"Prove me and see whether I will not open the windows of Heaven and pour out such a treasure as there shall not be room to hold it," promises the Lord.

God does pour out such rich blessings! God, the loving God, has already poured gifts into our life, day in and day out, abundantly, life, health, friends to cherish, mother and father to love, children to hold in our arms, bodily strength and intellect, work to do, home, food, clothing, our Church, and above all, the redeeming Savior. For all this the Christian can only say his thanks, forever say his thanks! The tithe is one way.

CHAPTER 7
Stewardship Sermon In Four Parts

The Parable Of The Pig Sty

(This sermon is divided into four parts and can be used as a single unit for a banquet speech or given as two sermons on two consecutive Sundays.)

St. Paul in 1 Corinthians 4:1-2 states, *"This is how one should regard us, as servants of Christ and stewrds of the mysteries of God . . . Moreover it is required of stewards that they be found faithful."*

Let me try to bring this statement into focus with a story. Young Joe was a husband of a lovely young wife and they had a wonderful baby daughter. All things seemed to be going along fairly well when the depression hit and Joe and many others had lost their jobs. Joe was desperate to try to find some kind of employment. It was decided that he would go out into the ranch country of North Dakota and offer himself as a ranch hand. Unfortunately there didn't seem to be any call for cowboys. After days of travel he settled down in a small cafe in Western Dakota. After lunch he asked the owner if he knew where there might be a job.

The owner said he knew of a place where they were looking for help. It was a ranch north of the town down in the Badlands which the natives referred to as the PIGSTY because all they raised at this ranch was pigs, hundreds of pigs. Because of the pigs no self-respecting cowboy would want to work there.

Joe took off for the "pigsty" and when he arrived, he was immediately put to work by the foreman in charge. He had a job, not a very pleasant job, but a job which would make it possible in a short time for him to bring his family together. His gratitude kept him diligent. He was a "sty-warden" of a bunch of pigs, as such, he was determined to do his best. He would be a good "sty-warden."

Days went by and one day the official owner of the ranch came to visit his holdings. As he drove into the ranch he didn't expect to find much change, but he was greatly surprised. He noticed that all the gates were on their hinges, the fences had been repaired, the outbuildings had been painted. All in all everything looked greatly improved.

He inquired of the foreman what had brought about all these improvements and the foreman told him about Joe. He was the most remarkable worker who tended to everything with steadfast care. The owner was impressed and said that he wished to meet this young man. Without revealing his identity, the owner went to where Joe was working on some machinery. Leaning over the fence he said, "My, you certainly must be very fond of pigs since you seem to take care of them in such a fine manner."

Joe looked up and smiled, "Stranger, you want to know something? I hate pigs, they stink. The reason I do my best so faithfully is that it is my way of saying 'thank you' to God for giving me the health to work so that I can support my family and thankful to the person who owns these pigs and entrusted them to my care."

The boss' mouth flew open, never in his life had he heard a "sty-warden" so faithful and trustworthy. That night as the boss retired to his bed, a smile came over his face because he had found an answer to a question that he had been pondering for some time. Recently he had purchased a calf camp down on the river bottom and he was wondering where he could find someone faithful enough to run it. As he went to sleep he knew exactly who it would be. He knew also what he was going to say to Joe. Words similar to those Jesus used in the parable of the talents, "Well done you good and faithful sty-warden, you have been found faithful over these little pigs, come I want to promote you and make you a partner over much."

Someone once suggested that "just maybe" this is the way the word steward and stewardship got started. The idea was that somewhere back in history there was a "sty-warden" so faithful that his boss raised him to greater positions of responsibility and riches. So outstanding was his faithfulness that the very name "sty-warden" was elevated to mean "a faithful manager of another's property and goods."

I think it was Margaret Seeback in her delightful little book titled *As A Woman Thinketh* suggested if this theory was true, then the very name "steward" was promoted from the pigsty to the royal throne of the Stuart Kings of England. Of course a greater promotion would be the way Jesus used it in His parable to express our relationship to God in response to His wonderful Grace.

Of course no one really knows that there is any truth to tying up the word "steward" to the word "sty-warden." True or not the basic idea that God isn't interested in "how much" or "how little" but "how faithful" we are with that which He has entrusted to us.

St. Paul in our text excitedly reminds the church member of Corinth how blessed they are, for they have been let in on the treasures of heaven, *"for you are stewards of the very mysteries of God."* He then goes on to remind them that because of this, the one thing required of them is that they be found faithful.

"The mysteries, mysteries of God." Something no one could ever guess until it was revealed to them through Christ and the Holy Gospel. Have you ever thought of it this way? Christianity, when you come right down to it, begins where every other religion in the world ends. In my study of the world religions, I have noticed that their goal is to find some kind of acceptance by whatever God they serve. They sacrifice everything to win acceptance. The beauty of Christianity begins by announcing to you the "Gospel," the "Good News," that you don't have to win God's acceptance and approval because you already have it. Recall the words of St. John, *"Behold what manner of love the Father has bestowed upon us in that we are children of God."* You are accepted. You are family. St. Paul of course reminds us, *"You are saved by Grace through faith and that is not of yourself lest anyone should boast."* He indicated that even our Faith *is God's gift to us.*

Luther saw it clearly when he wrote the explanation to the third article of the Apostle's Creed, "I believe that I *cannot believe* in Jesus Christ, my Lord, or come to Him, but the Holy Spirit (God) calls me through the Gospel (God) and enlightens me with His gifts and sanctifies me in one true faith in Christ." Understand it? Of course not! It is all God's doing and it is marvelous in our sight!

In the light of this truth, I always chuckle when I hear people say that they made a decision for Christ. They forget that it was Christ who made the decision to make us His own. Recall His words to His disciples, *"You did not choose me, but I chose you, and I chose you for a purpose that you might bear fruit and that the fruit might remain."*

I never fully understood that wonderful relationship offered to me until the day I became a father. As I held my baby daughter in my arms, I realized that my love actually helped create her, we loved her before we even saw her, and even though she might throw up on my new suit, or dent the fender on my car, as much as I might hate some of the things she might do, I would never stop loving her. It dawned on me then that Salvation through Christ means to be totally secure in the knowledge of His love. To me, salvation isn't so much a matter of being good, or even being saved, but of being HIS. Again Luther explains in the meaning to the second article of the creed, "He (Jesus) has redeemed (me), a lost and condemned creature." "Why?" "In order that I might be HIS OWN, live under him in his kingdom and serve Him . . ."

St. Paul stresses the same wonderful fact, *"I know Him and knowing Him, I am convinced that nothing, death or life, or principalities, or . . . shall ever be able to separate me from the love of God in Christ Jesus."* This is *Good News* and that is why it is called the Gospel.

Knowing this should make us realize the great privilege that has been given to us when we became a member of the Holy Christian Church, the Communion of Saints. The Book of Acts records, *"That the Lord added to the Church those that were being saved."* Again it is God's doing and it defies all explanation. It is all part of the very mystery of God and we have been entrusted with it.

We are Stewards of the very Mysteries of God and the one thing required of us is that we be found faithful.

Haven't you often wondered why we are so slow to live up to the wonder and the joy of so great a salvation? I guess most people are. Even the psalmist had to pray, *"Restore unto me the joy of your salvation."* **One day it dawned on me that one of the reasons our spirit lags short and we fail to be promoted into the joy of the Lord is due to the fact that we have failed to be found faithful with the "little pigs" God has entrusted into our care.** Following the analogy of our parable, we might label these "little pigs" simply, Time, Talent, and Treasures (wealth). Jesus Himself said that if we can't be trusted with earthly wealth, how can He ever trust us with heavenly riches. Let us take a look at some of these "little pigs" entrusted to our "Stewardship."

The Parable Of The Pig Sty — PART 2 — Time

Our conclusion from the previous chapter is simply stated. Maybe the reason we failed to be promoted into the rich joys of our salvation is due to the faithless way we have used God's other small gifts. The first of these might be the gift of TIME.

We have been given 168 hours of time since one week ago. That amounts to 10,080 minutes. Well might we ask ourselves just how many of those 10,080 minutes have been given to what Jesus referred to as the number one priority on the agenda of any sincere Christian, namely, WORSHIP. Jesus said, *"Seek first God and His righteousness."* Again and again the scripture enjoins us, *"To worship the Lord thy God, Him only shall you serve."*

These things are important as evidenced by the fact that Jesus did not neglect these little things. Scripture says of Jesus that He was always in the Synagogue on the Sabbath as was His custom. Again how often He surrounded His moments and His days with prayer. Golly, if Jesus in all of His sinlessness sought to be found faithful in these little acts of worship, how much should you and I in our sinfulness seek to be faithful here.

But worship is more than going to church and praying. It means a whole new lifestyle prompted by a whole new spirit. St. Paul says that when you are appreciative of the very mercies of God, then the only reasonable kind of worship is to give your very body as a living sacrifice. No longer a dead sacrifice to try to win God's approval but just out of sheer gratitude, live now with an eye to pleasing God. He said, *"Whatever you do in word, deed, do all you do in the Name of the Lord Jesus."* The moments of work and my pleasure can be entered into as worship.

The hymn said it so well. "Take my moments and my days, let them flow in endless praise." Consequently we don't just spend time, nor kill time . . . we use time to bring praise to His glory as we give our very lives to Him. This is worship at its best.

I recall reading a story many years ago that brought this truth home. It began when Jane, a young mother of three delightful little girls was told by her doctor that her days were numbered. Cancer had invaded her body. Those last days were given to prepare her husband and the family for the fact that she would soon be dead. Jane rested solidly on her faith in the Risen Christ and assured her family that when that day came she knew that she would be personally escorted to the Father's House, by the Father's own Son. The one thing she begged her husband to do after she was gone was to carry on with the girls just as if she was still there. Especially with

Christmas coming up. John promised to do his best. When Christmas came, John got the tree and the gifts and all the other things they always had. When Christmas morning came the three girls came dashing down the stairs to find loads of gifts under the tree. But as in the past, no one was allowed to open gifts until after Daddy read the Christmas Story about the baby Jesus and then everyone sang "Silent Night." Then with a rush the girls began unwrapping their gifts as their Daddy watched them with a mixture of joy and sorrow. At any rate he had kept his promise to Jane to make Christmas special as always. After the girls had opened all their gifts they came and surrounded their father.

"Daddy," they said, "We know how much you miss Mommy, and we do too. Now Daddy, we have something for you, Please close your eyes and don't peek until we say you can."

With that the three were off only to return in a few minutes.
"Okay Daddy, now you can look."

Low and behold standing before him were three little girls all dressed in bright turkish towels with other towels around their heads like turbins. They of course were acting out the story of the three wisemen.

In unison they said, "Daddy, we don't have any gold, we don't have any frankincense, and we don't have any myrrh, but Daddy, *we give you us . . . we give you us,*" and they rushed into the waiting arms of their father.

This is an expression of what worship can be at its best. Nothing can take the place of worship yet how faithless we often are in giving it priority in our days and nights and in the time allotted us. "Time" is just one of the "little pigs" God has given us. May we make the most of it while it is yet day.

Again there is more, other little pigs to consider. Let's look at Talent.

The Parable Of The Pig Sty — PART 3 — Talent

Our story continues and we shall look at another facet of our theme. Recall, the questions simply stated, maybe we aren't promoted into the great joy of the Gospel simply because we haven't been very faithful in our use of the other smaller gifts God has given us. Today, I would like to consider the gift of talent. From our Lord's teaching, everyone has some talent and he makes us aware it isn't the amount of talent a person has, but how faithful you use what talents you have been given.

Speaking from my experience of 42 years in the active ministry, I can say without reservation that some of the greatest work in the church has been contributed not by ten talented people, but by dedicated people with maybe only one or two talents but who faithfully used those talents to the Glory of God. Of course I have had some multi-talented people who have also done wonderful things, but they are few and far between.

In my ministry I have never believed anyone who said, "but Pastor I don't have many talents." It is right here that I take the time to tell them the story of one of the most remarkable women to grace the twentieth century. She is Dr. Ann Carlson, who spearheaded a wonderful hospital in North Dakota for crippled children. She has won an international reputation for her outstanding work.

Who is this multi-talented woman? Is she a woman with everything going for her? Hardly! She is a woman born without hands and feet. A person with three strikes against her. One thing she did have was the knowledge that God loved her and he expected her to use what little talent she did have — and use it she did. She got herself trained to become a doctor specializing in crippled children. Being crippled herself gave her the sensitivity to know what was needed to really help.

Joe Garagiola interviewed Dr. Carlson on the Today Show some years ago. He frankly admitted that he thought the interview would be filled with pity because of Dr. Ann's condition, but was he wrong. He admitted after the interview the only one he pitied was Joe Garagiola who had ten fingers and ten toes and yet did so little to help benefit humanity.

Whenever I address a church group I always remind them that there is enough talent in the room to turn the whole town upside down. Correction, to the contrary, there is enough talent to turn the town rightside up — it's already upside down.

I am sure every pastor has preached again and again about the many ways each person can serve in the congregation or community. There is the choir, Church Council, Sunday School Teaching, etc. One thing most of us forget is the stewardship of our personality. I had this graphically brought home when my saintly father died. The day of his funeral was a celebration of the Resurrection and Risen Lord. After the funeral, my family was together when suddenly there was a phone call. It was the hospital and the doctor informed me that one of the pastors that had been at the funeral had been in an accident and their little boy had been killed. Would I please come and help inform the family of the loss of their son? I was never so scared in all my life. Being only a student, what would I say? I don't mind telling you I prayed all the way to the hospital asking the Lord to give me the right words to say to bring comfort and strength. I went through with the task, but I must tell you I felt very much like a failure. Words didn't come easy, but I did my best. Well, to make a long story short, years went by and the Pastor mentioned above was the main speaker at one of our Anniversary Banquets. Before he went to the podium, he stopped behind my chair and putting his hands on my shoulder, he spoke. "Folks, before I begin my address I want to tell you something about your Pastor. Many years ago when our little boy was killed, this man came to our bedside to try to comfort us and bring us strength. Frankly, my wife and I don't remember a thing he said, but more important than anything he could have said was the fact that HE WAS THERE. That meant everything to us."

So often people will say, but Pastor I just don't know what to say. Maybe you don't have to say a thing but the fact that you cared enough to be there will say more than a million words. This is what I Call Stewardship of Personality.

Being there for Christ reminds me of the deaf man I had in my congregation who never missed attending church even though he couldn't hear a thing. He became an inspiration to many of us. So often we don't realize the power of our presence at worship in church. It has been said that by the very act of attending church every Sunday, it is in itself a silent sermon testifying to the fact we love the Lord Jesus enough to go into His house of prayer and being there for Him.

I often think of Christ on the cross and what a comfort it was to Him to see John and the three women standing by. There was nothing much they could say, but what a comfort it was to Him that THEY WERE THERE. In the parable of the talents, Jesus deliberately pointed out the fact that quite often the one talent people bury that one little talent, only to discover that either "you use it or you lose it."

There is always that temptation to "bug out" if you can't be king of the hill. That brings us to yet another problem. What about the multi-talented people in the church, which can include the pastor. There are positions of influence and power and as such they can easily turn a person's head. How easy it is to "Lord it over others." Even the disciples fell victim to this surge of power. Jesus warned them not to *"Rejoice that even the spirits were subject to them, but rather rejoice that their names were written in heaven."* The more we have the more responsible we are in using it not to "Lord it over others," but "to be the humble servant of all for the Lord's sake." If you have it, don't flaunt it, but use it to serve others that the name of Jesus may be praised.

Talents, "little pigs" that call us to faithful use of the same. One of the tragedies of the church is that we have forgotten how to encourage the aged and retired persons to use what God-given talents they still possess which, while serving others, gives a reverse blessing to make their own life meaningful. I like what someone once said, "retirement can be a drag when the fish aren't biting." I retired nine years ago but I must say I have been busy as can be with supply preaching, running the Lutheran World Relief project for the churches of the State, Meals on Wheels, etc. Golly, I find life exciting as long as the Lord allows me to be useful in His Name.

I shall always remember the story Margaret Runbeck tells in one of her accounts of the way the Jews tried to escape from the advancing Nazi troops in France. Members of the French Underground would lead groups of Jews over the mountains to a safe haven in Spain. One night a young mother came with a very small child and begged the guides to allow her to accompany the group. So desperate was her plea that she was included in the group to make the arduous journey. The mother and guide carried the child up the steep ascent together with thirty other climbers. About halfway up the mountain an old man fell to his knees, he was completely exhausted. He begged the guide to leave him there to die. The guide, however, reached over and gently lifted the old man to his feet. He then took the child and thrust her into the old man's arm with these words, "Look old man, whatever strength you have left you owe to all of us, so you carry the woman's child until you do drop dead." Three times that night this little scene was reenacted with some old folks that were ready to die. Again and again the guide repeated, "Look old one, whatever strength you have left you owe to all of us, you carry the woman's child until you do drop dead." The joyful results of it all, when morning came the group was safe in Spain and not one of the original thirty-three were dead. I think you catch the point. God has wonderful possibilities for the aged, even "tired talents" are still usable in his kingdom. AMEN.

Parable Of The Pigsty — PART 4 — The Littlest Pig — Money

I shall always remember the crazy ghost story my father used to tell. It seems that there was a beautiful home on the edge of town which the Realtors had difficulty in selling. People claimed that the house was haunted and everyone that moved into the house moved out the same night because they saw ghosts. In desperation, the real estate people made an offer to give a reward of $1,000 to anyone who would move into the house and remain there until morning, thus hoping to prove that the house wasn't haunted.

Well, there was a fine Christian Grandpa who felt that winning the $1,000 would help his grandson through college. So he offered to spend the night and he did and he won the $1,000.

Later that day as he met at the coffee shop with some of his cronies, they questioned him about the house. He confided in them that the house was haunted, but he was able to survive the night because he had a scheme. When the clock struck midnight, he looked up and sure enough there were those ghostly eyes peering out at him through the dark. Of course I was scared, but then I remembered what Luther said, "When you're afraid, sing." So I sang every great hymn I could remember but the eyes were still there. Then again I prayed every prayer I had been taught since youth, but those eyes were still there, so in desperation I quoted everything I remembered from scripture, but the ghostly eyes were still there. Then I had an idea. I leaned back in my chair and I addressed those ghosts and I said, "Look, I don't know what you want or who you are but I have sung for you, just like in church; I have prayed for you, just like in church; I have quoted scripture for you, just like in church, and now, just like in church I am going to pass the offering plates. Lo and behold, there was a loud zip, whoosh, and all the eyes were gone."

We laugh at such a story because somehow we know how skittish everyone is when it comes to talking about money in the church. I recall my first parish when one of my ranchers came to see me. He wanted to be honest with me and tip me off. "Look Pastor, you take care of the good book, the prayer book and hymn book, but please let me manage my pocketbook," he said. Little did he realize that he was giving me a beautiful opportunity to talk to him about the stewardship of money.

Very carefully I spoke up and said, "Joe, I am glad you stated your position the way you did and that is precisely why I would like to ask this question. Are you managing your pocketbook or is your pocketbook managing you? I'm glad you used the word 'manage' for it is a way of telling me you believe that what you possess isn't really yours but God has entrusted you to use it wisely according to His plan. It also recognizes the fact that you realize that the day will come when you and I will have to have an audit and give account to the real owner of all we possess, the very God who has given us the ability to make money." I think Joe was a little bit stunned by what I had to say. I am happy to this day that I had the courage to say it because I am happy to report Joe took it to heart and became very generous in the support of the Lord's work.

How do we manage our pocketbooks? According to the newspaper last week, American's are giving a little more than 2 percent of their income to the support of church and charity. Reports have it that American's gave more than 3.4 percent of their incomes during the height of the depression in 1930. It seems the more we have the less we give.

I was dumbfounded to read that Lutherans didn't fare better. A report made recently stated that only 21 percent of our people practiced proportionate giving. That means that 79 percent are giving haphazardly, without plan or forethought — tossing in leftovers — giving what they please, when they please, and especially if they are pleased.

What a horrible way to treat God who long before the foundation of the world, pledged to give us through Christ the precious gift of salvation. He pledged it and in the fullness of time that pledge was paid in full on a Cross in His own blood.

St. Paul says that if we are Christians at all, the very least we can do to express our love and gratitude to God for all of his benefits to us, is to be REGULAR, DELIBERATE AND PROPORTIONATE IN OUR GIVING.

Paul writes, "Let a person lay aside . . ." That suggests planned giving. After all your giving is not a witness to your profit and loss, but a testimony to your love. Remember when you fell in love how much thought and planning went into finding just the right gift.

Paul continues, "Let a person lay aside *ON THE FIRST DAY OF THE WEEK . . .*" That suggests *REGULARITY*, certainly anything less would not be an appropriate gift for a God who daily provides me with all the necessary things for life. The very suggestion that it should be weekly, suggests it is part of our weekly worship.

And last but not least, it should be PROPORTIONATE giving. God doesn't expect us to give what we don't have. He is more than fair, He is generous to a fault. He asks that we give percentage wise as He has prospered us. Our government isn't shy about demanding 28 to 35 percent or upward, but God isn't greedy. Long ago He said to His people of Israel, make a tithe, 10 percent but with this stipulation. Make it the first 10 percent. There is reason for that request. It helps us put God where he belongs, first on the list of our priorities. Recall how He said, *"When it comes to God or money (mammon) seek first God then all these other things will be added unto you as well."* That's His promise and a person is a fool to ignore it. It is His way of making us good managers of our pocketbooks.

I think of that day when Jesus was surrounded by 5,000 hungry people. Jesus turned to His disciples and said, *"How are you going to manage? This He said to test them because He himself knew what He was going to do."*

That very story should suggest to us why we are forever put to the test to see if we do trust God before we trust wealth. He wants us to take His word for it when He said, *"Try me, see if I won't open windows of heaven and pour down such a blessing you will not be able to receive it all."* You see, God has some big promotions in store for us but he must know whether we are capable to receive them.

Talk about "little pigs," money is one of the cheapest of all of God's gifts to us and He wants to know whether we can manage these small things before moving us into more grandiose plans. I would put it this way — IF GOD CAN'T TRUST ME WITH THE CASH, DARE HE TRUST ME WITH A CROWN? Jesus of course put it more pointedly when he warned us to the effect that if we can't be found faithful with earthly wealth, how can we expect to share heavenly treasures.

There is an old song that said, "Little Things Mean A Lot." In any case we should have learned that we are called upon to be good "sty-wardens" not only of the mysteries of God, but stewards of the little things like time, talent and treasure that God has entrusted to our care. May God grant us the joy of hearing him say, *"Well done, thou good and faithful steward, you have been found faithful over little, come I want to make you ruler over much, enter into the joy of your Lord."*

CHAPTER 8
How Are You Going To Manage?

A Sermon Before Pledging

Beloved of the Lord . . . I must tell you how happy I am to be here again. Since I was here three years ago, a lot has taken place. When I reached my sixty-seventh birthday I decided to retire. To some that is a frightening experience. Many find themselves in a state of limbo. They told a humorous story about me at my retirement party. I'd like to share it with you. According to the story I had a dream that a wicked witch turned me into a talking frog. A curse was laid on me so that I would remain a frog forever unless a beautiful woman would come along and kiss me. Desperately I called my wife Dorothy, "Dorothy, come and kiss me." She came and picked me up and stood there looking at me. I shouted at her to hurry up and kiss me so I could return. Yet, she hesitated. Again I cried, "What are you waiting for?" Slowly she replied, "I'm deliberating and trying to decide what is more valuable, a talking frog or a retired pastor?" Evidently her better nature won out and here I am a retired pastor, doing the very thing I want to do — preach.

Fall Preaching

I do love to preach, particularly in the Fall when I am invited to church after church like yours to talk to people about some of the most important things in the world. Of course Number One is GOD and the glory of the Gospel of Jesus Christ, and the Second is Money and helping people establish the proper relationship between the two. Many people find it difficult to listen to sermons about money and many pastors find it extremely difficult to speak about money. I don't. I find it exhilarating and exciting. Nothing thrills me more than to preach to a congregation and discover that following the sermon they generously increase their giving by 20 to 25 percent because they finally look upon their giving as a joyful act of worship and not a chore.

I believe that people need to hear sermons about money and the place where it fits into the Christian's life. My role model for such preaching is the Master Himself. We are reminded that He had more to say about money than He did about heaven, hell, and prayer. Just check the number of parables that have money and material possessions as a central theme. When Jesus walked among us He immediately spotted the real reason why so many people were cracking up. They literally were "worrying themselves sick" because they were trying to serve two masters. You guessed it, God and Mammon. One has to become dominant over the other and the question resolves itself into, "What will it be God or gold?"

Choked To Death With A Necklace

Jesus was correct in his diagnosis of our situation that is why he spent an inordinate amount of His teaching showing us how the obsessive love of money coupled with our absolute trust in wealth can grind the very life and love out of our existence.

A case in point is that graphic story of Guy de Maupusant called *The Necklace*. Basically it was about a young government clerk and his wife Matilda. He came home one evening all excited because he had received an invitation to an exclusive fancy ball. They both were thrilled to be included but their joy was short lived because Matilda said she couldn't go because she didn't have anything worth while to wear to the ball. To solve the problem they used up most of their small savings in order to purchase just the right dress. Again the joy was short lived because Matilda didn't have the proper jewelry to wear with the new dress. Finally they decided that she should borrow a fine piece of jewelry from one of her rich friends. The friend did lend her a magnificent necklace with diamonds. The couple went to the ball and had a wonderful time. As they returned home, Matilda discovered that the necklace was missing. Frantically they searched everywhere to find it but to no avail. The only thing they could think of to do was to purchase a replacement. Of course it meant mortgaging their entire future. They found a necklace similar to the one they had lost and they bought it and returned it to the friend. They had to give up their home, forsake the idea of having children, and both worked long hours to try to meet the payments. Years went by and finally Matilda's health gave out. All she could do was sit and sun herself in the park. Then one day her rich friend went by and Matilda made herself known to her friend. Her friend hardly recognized Matilda because she was so thin and sickly. Her friend inquired about her condition and then Matilda told the story of the lost necklace and how they had purchased another to replace it and how they had worn themselves out trying to make the payments. It was then the rich friend turned ashen white and exclaimed, "Oh my dear woman, the necklace that I loaned you was paste."

Profitless Profits

"What shall it profit a person if they should gain the whole world and in the process lose their very soul." Recall the parable of the rich man that kept building bigger and bigger barns to hold all of the wonderful wealth he possessed, or rather which possessed him. He thought he had it made, but our Lord's appraisal was, *"You fool, this very night your soul shall*

be required of you." The man loved money and used God when in reality we are to love God and use money as stewards of God's grace. St. Paul says it is the inordinate love of money that is the cause of all kinds of evil and leads to a sin that is so great that it clinched the whole of the ten commandments and that sin is "covetousness." It is a sin that warns us to watch the desires of our heart. A greedy heart can absolutely destroy your ability to know any peace or contentment or happiness. If there is anything Jesus wants us to share it is the joy that can be ours when GOD COMES FIRST and we rely on Him. It is foolish for us to put our trust in money and the things money can buy for there still are thieves and rust and falling stock markets that can make us pay for everything we have with what we are.

Priorities

No wonder Jesus encouraged us to "Seek FIRST God and his righteousness and then all these other things will be ADDED TO YOU as well." After all, your heavenly Father knows that you need all of these things. He has a way of providing. Look at the birds of the air, they can't even build a barn, but your God takes care of them. Don't you trust Him enough to seek Him first?

Right now on this Loyalty Sunday God is somehow putting us to the test. He is giving the opportunity to show our love and trust in Him even when it comes to the matter of our wealth. Do you recall that day when more than five thousand hungry people were present and Jesus had compassion on them and He turned to His disciples and He asked them this question, *"How are you going to manage? This He said to test them because He Himself knew what He was going to do."* It was then that Phillip said, "There is a lad here with a few loaves and fishes." So far, so good, but then he spoiled it all by saying, *"But what is that among so many?"* He is like most of us forever overstating our poverty. Jesus commands them to have the crowd sit down and I'm sure you recall the rest. The biggest thrill came that day when a boy ran home and shouted to his mother, "Golly Mom, you should have seen the miracle Jesus and I did today, we fed five thousand." That boy knew the incredible joy that can be ours when in the name of love for Jesus we learn the secret of giving that is pleasing in His sight.

Attitudes That Attain

You know it and I know it from our experience. When you give a gift or you receive a gift, more important than the gift is the spirit and attitude in which it is given. You can see from this that the most important question every member of the congregation asks themselves is, "Just why do I give?" I hope that you aren't giving to try to meet the budget. In all of my congregations, we never even made up a budget until after we had received all of our pledges. Budgets are primarily a guide to the Church Council on how to spend the money wisely. Even if just one person's contribution entirely underwrites the total current budget, that is never an excuse for the rest to stop giving generously. We don't give to the budget or a program, nor do we simply give to the church. I give to support the church, the whole church, both local and mission-wise, primarily because I love my Lord. Giving is my opportunity to prove the realness of my faith in Him. He taught me how to give by His example when He gave Himself for me.

Last Word . . . Give

St. Paul learned that lesson well and that is why on his last journey, his last word to the church of Ephesus was, *"Remember the word of the Lord Jesus how He said it is more blessed to give than to receive."* I used to think that was stretching it a bit but then it dawned on me one Christmas when my wife reminded me that we both got a bigger kick out of the gifts we gave our children and our grandchildren than we did in the gifts we received. Basically, I think we all are very selfish at heart and it takes some real effort and exercise to develop the "give muscle" in our hearts. Here again God has not left us helpless. Long ago He established a spiritual exercise called "The Tithe." Here we are invited to set aside at least 10 percent of our income as an act of worship. It should be set aside FIRST. Love never throws in its leftovers. Love plans its giving. Many forget that all that we are and all that we have are gracious gifts from God and we are tempted to lose sight of the fact that we are responsible to God in just how we use all of His gifts to us. Because we are prone to forget this, God declared a long time ago, "the tithe belongs to me" and He further indicated that when we withhold the tithe we are literally robbing Him. He didn't say that because He was greedy, far from it. He is vitally concerned that we get over this greedy attitude and our absolute foolish trust in the almighty dollar — Mammon.

Try It, You'll Like It

If you have never tried to tithe, why not try it now? Try it for a month or two. *Even God encourages you to "Try it says the Lord and I tell you I will open up the windows of heaven and pour on you such blessing you won't be able to receive it all."* Remember this isn't a Megabucks Lottery with one chance in 13,000,000. This is your Heavenly Father declaring his never failing love. I know you feel that you have trouble making ends meet even now. How in heaven's name will I ever be able to manage if I take the first dollar from every ten dollars I earn and give it as my thank offering to the Lord? But that is just the point. In order to do it, YOU WILL HAVE TO TRUST GOD to manage it for you. When you are ready to take the plunge, you will soon say with thousands of others who have tried it before, "Wow, why didn't I start this practice long ago?" You see, money and tithing are only the implements, the keys to start the motor running. Once you discover the joy that comes from a trusting giving heart, you will recognize that this sermon isn't about raising money, but about raising people into the joy of the Lord as faithful stewards of His manifold grace. The scripture declares, *"No one that ever trusts Him will be disappointed."*

Now Its Your Turn

In your hand you have a pledge card to say very much the same thing. Here is an opportunity to prove the reality of your faith. Remember long before you were born God pledged your salvation and then on a cross He paid that pledge in full. Now it is your turn. Let us pray . . . . .

*Lord give me faith to see the Kingdom's need
Increase my faith that I may give
Without one taint of greed
these fruits of grace.
O give me faith that ripens into Christian Love
to Earthlings here and to my God above.*
AMEN

CHAPTER 9
A Dime's Worth Of Trust

A Banquet Speech For Pledging

It is good to be here and share with you some thoughts about God and our response to His goodness. Let me begin by telling you about a crazy dream I had. In this dream I saw myself before the gate of heaven. I knocked and a voice asked, "Who's there?" I told him that it was Genszler from Waukesha, Wisconsin. The voice then asked, "Are you mounted?" Of course I wasn't mounted so I was turned away. As I came down the hill I ran into Pastor Jones (*use local pastor's name here*). I told him about my experience and that he shouldn't waste his time since he wasn't mounted.

Pastor Jones spoke up and said, "Well, Bill, if you are willing I think I can get both of us into heaven. All you have to do is get down on all fours and I will climb on your back and thus we both will gain entrance to heaven." It sounded like a fairly good idea so I did as Pastor Jones suggested.

When we got back to the gate of heaven the voice again asked, "Who's there?" My friend answered, "Pastor Jones of Milwaukee." Again the question, "Are you mounted?" "Yes, I am mounted," replied Pastor Jones. "O.K. then," came back the reply. "Tie your jackass outside and come on in."

That little story reminds me of an unusual story in the Bible concerning a donkey. You recall the day that Jesus wanted to ride into Jerusalem. We call it Palm Sunday. When they came to Bethpage He sent two of His disciples into the village opposite them and immediately they would find an ass tied, and a colt with her. The disciples were to untie the animals and bring them to Jesus. Jesus told them that if anyone questioned them they were merely to reply, *"The Lord has need of them,"* and immediately the owner would release them into the hands of the disciples.

What a perfect illustration this was of the true meaning of Faith and Trust in the Lord. Christ's very wish became their command. They put God above all things including their material possessions. They trusted Him.

The big question each of us must ask, Do we trust Him? Do we even give Him a DIME'S WORTH OF TRUST when it comes to our giving and sharing of our earthly wealth? Just where does MONEY fit into our agenda? Is it first, second, or last in our scheme of things? Let me help sharpen our vision by considering a humorous story I learned from my father.

There was a story about a young beautiful school teacher who moved to a midwest town. It didn't take the banker long to court this lovely lady. After a few months they were married. Because of his wealth, she became very rich. Years went by and then one day her husband was killed in a plane crash and she was single again. But not for long, for the owner of the local show house started to court her and after several months they were wed. Years went by and then he suffered a fatal heart attack and our lady was single again. With two great losses in her life, she took to religion. She actually ended up playing the organ in her church. It so happened that they got a new minister and he was handsome and he was single. You guessed it! In a matter of time they were wed. They lived happily for about five years when he was killed in a fatal car wreck. She was single again, but not for long. The local funeral director took a liking to her and after a year he won her hand in marriage.

One day when our lady was having lunch with some of her lady friends, one of them spoke up and said, "Darling, you have been married four times, first it was the banker, then the

Itinerary

6/1 (NW 0287)
LV: BWI @ 9:35 A
AR: Detroit @ 11:02 A
LV: Detroit @ 12:30 p (0933)
AR: Los Angeles @ 2:19 p

6/8 LV: L.A. @ 8:30 A (NW 932)
AR: Detroit @ 3:48 p
LV: Detroit @ 5:16 p (1111)
AR: BWI @ 6:49 p

Melva Giles
1-805-273-0453

show man, and then the minister, and now, the undertaker. How do you explain such an assortment?

Laughingly she replied, "Easy, one for the MONEY, two for the SHOW, three to get READY, and four to GO."

When you come right down to it, her remarks could easily become our outline for my banquet speech tonight. Let's take a look at it.

One For The Money

Wait just one minute. When it comes to stewardship, should money come first? We have been led to believe that you shouldn't talk too long or too loudly about money in the church. Didn't Jesus Himself point out that in our giving we shouldn't let the left hand know what the right hand was doing? Many people fail to see the point that Jesus was making. He suggests that our giving should be generous and not cautious and calculating.

Many people are forever cautiously trying to figure out how little they can give rather than how much they should give. Again, many people will say that giving is a very private and personal affair and it is nobody's business but their own. How often people will say that if you get the heart of the people set right, automatically money and material possessions will take their proper place.

I suppose we have been led to believe these things simply because we want to believe them. There is just enough truth in them to make them sound logical but just enough lie in them to make them a lot of soft soap.

It is important for us to look at Jesus and discern just where money was placed in His life. Let's face it. His very first temptation in the wilderness dealt with this issue of money and the things money could buy. It was a question of Bread, material possessions, money, and things money could buy. It is interesting that the slang of a past generation said "Lay some bread on me." By this they definitely mean "money." Luther also speaks of "Daily Bread" as including our wealth, health, family, food, and all things of life which our Heavenly Father knows that we need.

Christ's temptation was exactly the same one we face everyday, the temptation to trust the supposed security of earthly wealth more than we trust the providential care of a Gracious God. Jesus kept His priorities straight and overcame the temptation, but the very fact that it appeared first is a demonstration that money, bread, wealth, does have a way of pushing itself to the forefront in our considerations so that we are prone to trust GOLD rather than GOD. It is because we are all so tempted to be lead astray by the MIDAS touch that Jesus goes out of His way in one parable after another to point out the pitfalls of wealth. I wonder if you ever noticed that Jesus has more to say about money than He has to say about prayer, Heaven or Hell. He stresses the fact that the way we think about money and its uses has a revealing way of SHOWING exactly where we stand in our TRUST RELATIONSHIP TO GOD. I think we can safely say, ONE for the MONEY, TWO for the SHOW.

Two For The Show

It is very evident from scripture that the acid test concerning our trust in Christ comes right at this juncture. Recall the penetrating event when a rich young ruler came to Jesus seeking the gift of eternal life. Here was a young person who was a very paragon of virtue. Jesus was impressed to the point where it says that Jesus looked on him and loved him. Then came the acid test. Did he trust God more than his riches? Would he be willing to give it away and follow Christ? We are told he miserably failed the test and he went away sorrowful because he had great possessions. The fact of the matter is, his possessions had possessed him.

Do you see why Jesus is so tough on us concerning our wealth? He had seen money destroy the faith and trust of those

He loved. You can almost sense the pathos in His voice as He emphatically stated, *"Look, you cannot serve God and Mammon. It is impossible to serve two masters. You must place one over the other."* If we paraphrase it, we might say, "You either give God your dime's worth of trust over the management of your pocketbook or your pocketbook will choke the life of God out of your soul. Either you trust God or worry yourself sick about tomorrow.

It is "one for the money" and "two for the show." St. Paul states it when he wrote to the Church in Corinth and reminded them, "Your very giving proves the reality of your faith, and that means that others will thank God you practice the Gospel that you profess to believe in." You see, it shows! Money tells a lot. One day Jesus answers a question by saying, *"Show me a penny."* To us he might say, "Let me look at your check stubs or your credit card bills and it will show me where your heart is."

It is always an embarrassment to those people who are always so hush, hush about the giving of money to learn how Jesus views the whole thing. True giving is indeed a very *personal* thing but it is seldom *private*. Recall how Jesus took His disciples to the Narthex of the Temple to deliberately show them how people gave beyond the call of duty. They were impressed by the generosity of several rich people. Then came the poor widow. She didn't have a social security check coming in every month. All she had were two small coins. They could have been the price of her supper. She is low on coin, but rich in trust. She joyfully drops the coins in the trumpet, confident that God would provide, therefore she refused to worry herself sick about tomorrow. She would let her money *show her real love and trust in God*. Yes, "one for the money," "two for the show," "three to get ready."

Three To Get Ready

There is a silly old story about the man who got up to the gate of heaven and was met by St. Peter who questioned the man about his claim on heaven. The man related that he was a decent sort of a fellow all his life. He never beat his wife, he wouldn't hurt a fly. He simply believed in "live and let live."

St. Peter looked up and said, "Is that all! Didn't you even contribute money to the poor?"

"Indeed I did," he replied, "I remember giving a bum a dime for a cup of coffee back in the depression."

Saint Peter said, "I think I will have to check with the Boss about this."

He called on the phone to the Lord about this man.

When the conversation was over, the man asked, "What did the Lord say?"

St. Peter replied, "He said give him back his dime and tell him to go to hell."

We laugh at such a ridiculous story but the truth of the matter is, Jesus told of a similar event in the parable of the talents.

When it came to the man who buried his one talent, Jesus didn't say, "Give him back his talent and then cast him out."

On the contrary, He did say, "Take that one talent away from the idle rascal and then toss him out." When you see it in that light, it doesn't sound very funny and truly it isn't. Jesus made no secret of the fact that everyone of us will be audited as to the use or the abuse of the many talents God gave us to manage. It isn't how much or how little, but how faithful we have been as stewards of His grace. Shockingly put, "If God can't trust me with the cash, dare he trust me with a crown?"

I sometimes think that God instituted the tithe to help us keep our priorities straight. Thus he requested each person to begin honoring God with their substance and wealth, by setting aside at least the FIRST TEN PERCENT of their income as an ACT OF WORSHIP. It was proof that we would give God at least a dimes worth of our trust, *first*. The first dime out of every dollar. Jesus never repudiated the tithe as a reasonable first step in rendering to God what is God's. Of course if you have never tried to tithe, it might "scare the

Devil" out of you and that might be just what you need to do. The thing about tithing is the wonderful discovery you make in trusting God. You will find that He is faithful and your friend. As the Bible states, *"Nobody who ever trusts Him will ever be disappointed."* He promises to open heaven's windows and rain down such a blessing you won't be able to receive it all.

Four To Go

"ONE for the MONEY," "TWO for the SHOW," "THREE to get READY," and "FOUR to GO." The word GO is the first two letters of the word GOD. Jesus' prescription for the total enrichment of life both now and forever is to, *"Seek first God and His righteousness."* Then, money will never master us or possess us and destroy us, but will become our servant to do good unto all people especially unto those of the household of faith. If I remember correctly, St. Paul said the same thing. I know that many people say, "You can't take it with you! You never saw a U-Haul following a hearse?" True, but according to Jesus you can send it on ahead. Jesus suggests that you can transform cash into friends for the Lord. *"Make friends with Mammon of unrighteousness."* Not a bad idea. "Lay up treasures in heaven where the Dow Jones averages won't fold, and rust and thieves won't rip you off." Invest wealth in those things that have eternal significance.

Who can forget the graphic picture of the Last Judgment. Pray the Lord that we might hear His glorious accolade. *"Come blessed of my father, I was hungry and you fed me, I was naked and you clothed me, ..."* I'm sure you know the rest.

FOUR to GO. We can never forget his commission to *"Go into the world and make disciples . . ."* Of course it will take money to do just that and you and I have been given the same. Will we hear His request. *"Just tell them that the Lord has need of them."*

Now it is your turn. You have been given a pledge card. You have an opportunity right now to prove to yourself that you do trust God above all things.

Let us pray:
  Lord, the time has come
    to prove the reality of my faith in you.
  May the wonders of your Grace
    set my heart aflame with generosity and trust
  as I pledge to support your Holy Church.
    May Your Word so abide in my heart
    that it might bring forth fruit unto eternal life
                                    AMEN.

CHAPTER 10
Beyond Gratitude

Indelible Impression — Thank Offering Sermon

The sun was setting over Green Lake. All the campers had sung *Day is Dying in the West*. The speaker rose to tell us a story that I shall never forget even though I can't remember who the speaker was. The story went something like this.

It was night and the streets of Jerusalem were empty save for a solitary figure and that person was Jesus. As he turned the corner He noticed an open doorway with light streaming forth through the portico. As He drew closer He could hear the sound of music and drunken laughter. Looking into the house He saw Simon as the host of the banquet. Jesus also saw the sheer extravagance of this baccilanian brawl. Jesus quietly made His way through the crowd of drunken revelers until He stood directly behind Simon. Gently but firmly Jesus laid His hand on Simon's shoulder.

As Simon turned toward Jesus, Jesus asked, "Simon, why do you live like this?"

Simon's response was, "How else should I live, my Lord? Don't you remember, Lord, I was a hopeless leper and you came along and healed me. With this new found health I returned to my family and my business and I struck it rich so that I have more than enough. My Lord, how else should I live?"

Jesus was too sick of heart to answer Simon and so He returned to the darkness of the street. Shortly He heard the tinkle of tiny bells as a woman of the street raced by Him. It was evident that she would sell her body for a few coins. She had no sooner past on down the street when Jesus was aware of a handsome young man following her. His eyes aflame with lust and fornication in his heart. Jesus recognized the young man and reached out and stopped him in his flight.

Jesus spoke to him and asked, "My son, why do you live like this?"

Again the young man recognized Jesus and answered, "My Lord, don't you remember? I was born blind and never could see the beauty of earth or the sky, or the face of my loved ones and then you came along and heard my plea for help. You reached out and touched my eyes and behold I could see. My Lord, how else should I live?"

Again Jesus was too sick of heart to answer. In the last scene we find Him near the gate of the city. There He finds a woman at the edge of the cliff. She is crying and you can tell from her tearful mumbling that she is contemplating suicide.

Jesus touches her shoulder and asks again, "My dear, why do you live like this?"

Looking up she recognizes Jesus and she blurts out, "My Lord, don't you remember? I was dead and you came to my father's house and raised me from the dead and you gave me life. Since you gave it to me I figured it was mine to do with as I please and so I played fast and loose with life and now I find that life has played fast and loose with me and I guess there is only one way to end my misery. My Lord, how else should I live?"

I suppose we could go on and on with illustration after illustration featuring these small tragic follies. Of course, we say this was only a make-believe story or was it?

Nine Lives Lived Up

The scripture tells a similar story about ten lepers that came to Jesus for help, and they weren't disappointed. We are told that Jesus told them to go and show themselves to the Priest, the local health authority. Even as they went they found they were healed. I can imagine just how happy and thrilled these men were. They had been rescued from sure and certain death. Gratitude must have flooded their hearts. Who wouldn't be grateful for such a gift? Yes, I'm sure all ten of them were more than grateful but that is as far as it went with nine of them. Nine of them could only think of the joy of returning home to their families, their businesses. I imagine they often spoke about how really grateful they were for running into the man, Jesus. But nothing came of it. Someday I should like to write a novel and call it "Nine Lives Lived Up" and tell about these nine men who were given a second crack at life and blew it. Their's was gratitude that grates.

Gratitude That Goes Into Gear — Thanksgiving

I am sure that the tenth leper was just as anxious to get home to his wife and children and his business, as were the other nine. All of these wonderful things had been returned to him because of the love and concern of a stranger named Jesus. Surely, just plain decency would demand that the first order of business would be to return to Him who had given him a second chance at life and thank Him for His help. Of course this would take time and effort to do just that but isn't that exactly the difference between the plain swimming feeling of gratitude and the actual effort of rendering of thanks.

The Psalmist expressed it perfectly when he stated, *"What shall I render unto my God for all the benefits to me?"* And the answer came clear, "I will render the SACRIFICES of thanksgiving . . ." I will do something to show I am really grateful, something that will cost me something in time, talent, and treasure. The Psalmist lists several things he wants to do to show his appreciation. Among them he says, *"I will enter His courts with praise (he will go to church), I will pay my vow before the whole congregation, I will bring an offering.*" Not a collection, but an offering, something that costs me something. I want it to show my love for God and my thankfulness for all His benefits to me.

The Hallmark Of The Christian

Martin Luther in the explanation to the first article of the Apostles Creed, speaks of all of God's gifts to us, not that we deserve them, but simply because of His divine goodness and mercy, all for which we are duty bound to THANK, PRAISE, serve and obey Him. When you come right down to it everything on this earth shows forth the glory of God and all His creatures testify to His goodness. The only cantankerous creature in the bunch is the human being. We alone are the only ones that turn our backs on Him and when we do, we miss the greater joy He has for us which He shared with the one that came back to thank Him. Recall that greater blessing with eternal promise, *"Go your way, your faith has made you whole."*

I recall a slogan I once read that spoke of the ungrateful thankless person. It read, "They are like so many hogs eating acorns under a tree and never once look up to see where they are coming from." This thought found expression in a poem I wrote many years ago. It first appeared in the magazine published by the National Council of Churches called, *Stewardship Facts*.

Thanks — Living

WHAT WOULD YOU THINK OF —
    A mirror lacking image or a sunlight minus light or
    A Rainbow without color or a star as black as night.

WHAT WOULD YOU THINK OF —
    Food that is always tasteless or a rose without a smell or
    A fire that is always chilly or rain that never fell.

WHAT WOULD YOU THINK OF —
A word without a meaning or a man without a face or
A symphony that's soundless or a love that shares no Grace
'Tis too horrible to picture such a weird and senseless scheme
but it isn't half as crazy as a Thankless human being
Whose life reflects no glory to their gracious God above
Who selfish live and never give to share the Savior's love.

No Substitute For Thanksgiving

The longer I live the more I am convinced that gratitude is no substitute for the actual Giving of Thanks. This can be amply illustrated by the way we Americans observe Thanksgiving Day. Here is a day set aside nationally for people to render thanks to Almighty God for all of our blessings. Oh yes, our TV and newspapers talk about all the things we should be grateful for, yet when Thanksgiving day comes our churches are more than half empty. It just seems that the more we have been given the less thankful we are.

Well might our Lord ask, "Why do you live like this?" Pray God that we will not foolishly reply, "Lord, how else should I live?" Instead may we return to Him with Thanksgiving and find His additional gifts of grace to make us whole so our lives may show forth His praise forever.

CHAPTER 11
The Chance Of A Lifetime

Banquet Sermon For Capital Fund Campagin

Thank you Mr. Toastmaster. That was an excellent introduction. In fact, I only heard one that was better and that was one I wrote myself. HA! All kidding aside let me tell you a true story of one of the most original introductions I ever received. It happened at one of our churches in Escanaba, Michigan.

The toastmaster for the occasion was a blind lawyer.

He said, "Since I was to introduce Pastor Genszler to the congregation I thought I should gather up some information about him. I stopped to see the pastor of my church who began listing Pastor Genszler's many accomplishments. Well, the list was so long I knew that I would never be able to remember it so I asked the pastor to put it on tape." The toastmaster went on, "And then I had my secretary punch it out in Braille cards which I hold in my hand. It was a most impressive list. Unfortunately, as I was entering the banquet hall tonight, I dropped the cards and several people walked over them and flattened all the Braille points and now as I run my hand over the cards I find that I am unable to 'say one good thing about this man'!!" That really was the best introduction I ever received.

The Chance Of A Lifetime

You know that there are a great many people that are given the privilege of building their own home. Have you ever realized that not everyone is given the supreme privilege of building the Lord's House? King David had a great desire to build the temple to the Glory of God, but God said, "No." It was said that David had dipped his hands in blood too often. God declared that though David could not build the temple, this privilege would be given to his son, Solomon.

Of course there are many people who have no desire to build anything to the Glory of God because they have no taste for God. They remind me of two thieves that stole two sacks of what they thought was rock salt from an airport in Abijan, Africa. Salt is highly valued in that portion of the world. When they got back to their villages they shared the salt with other families. Strangely enough the salt did nothing to flavor their food, so they dumped the majority of the loot in the village dump. It was a few days later that the government authorities came and arrested the thieves for stealing two bags of small industrial diamonds worth more than $110,000.

More than one person has missed the real value of things spiritual. But to you who are spiritually alive, it remains a compliment of God to be allowed to do His work, whether it is sending missionaries to some distant shore, or build a building made with wood and stone where His word can be preached and where the Sacraments can be administered to you and your family.

THINK OF IT THIS WAY — YOU ARE GIVEN A PRIVILEGE THAT WAS DENIED EVEN THE AUTHOR OF THE 23RD PSALM. Don't despise this high and holy task set before you. You have been chosen to do a specific task and in a very singular way you can bring praise to His Glory to build His House of Worship.

You and I live in an age when there are many who would tear down the House of the Lord and discredit the teaching of God's Word. Recent history will testify to the fact that where people despise or neglect the House of the Lord they also end up with no home of their own.

Light House Keeping

This is a true story of a small church on the coast of England. One day it was totally destroyed by a hurricane. Since there were so few people attending the little church, it was decided not to rebuild. Delegates of the British Admiralty came to inquire whether the people intended to rebuild their little church on the coast.

When the people said, "No," the admiral said, "Then we will rebuild it. For that church spire is on all of our navigational maps and charts and is a landmark to guide our ships."

Somehow, I feel that our churches are landmarks to guide our people to safety. Someone has said that the churches of our land are the grist mills of strength and security for our life and community together. Let us always remember that the Church of Jesus Christ is the only institution that has a vital concern about our spiritual welfare. It is the only institution that is concerned with us as persons and children of God and it is the only institution that makes moral sense because it is concerned with bringing our lives into harmony with the nature of God. When you and I are called upon to build the House of the Lord, we are actually establishing a "Beachhead for Good" in our midst.

And The Walls Came Tumbling Down

We're alarmed when we hear about violent earthquakes that shake our world. Thousands are killed during the event, but are we equally alarmed by the earthquake that is shaking our nation to pieces. Recently researchers stated that a large percentage of our population fear that they will become victims of violence or crime. The events of the past few years have revealed spiritual wickedness in every walk of life from the highest to the lowest. Crime, corruption, violence, cheating, and greed have eroded every corridor of life. To make matters worse, gambling has become an addictive way of life for hosts of Americans. They never realize that this lust to get something for nothing is to risk what we have been given is an open violation of the responsibility of faithful stewardship of God's gifts to us. Ours is an age in which nothing seems sacred. We have put profits and pleasures ahead of God, people, and principles.

It reflects the same set of conditions that the prophet of old found when he proclaimed, *"The people felt no sense of responsibility for one another but each continued to live according to what they thought was right in their own eyes."*

They fast became victims of the blind leading the blind and they all fell into the ditch. Their's was a horizontal morality detached from any solid point of truth outside themselves.

Horizontal Morality

It was Dr. Paul Scherer that first illustrated this questionable kind of ethics. One day a boy came home from school and he asked his father, "Dad, what is ethics?"

The father answered, "Son, ethics has to do with morals."

"But Dad, what are morals?"

"Well son," he said, "I can't define it but I can illustrate it. It is something like this. Your Uncle Jake and I run this clothing store. One day a man comes in and buys a tie worth $3.00 and he hands me a ten dollar bill. All during the transaction we are both talking about the football game. Without thinking I give him $2 in change. He leaves the store without realizing that I had shortchanged him. I don't realize that I have shortchanged him until a few seconds after he is gone. Now, this is where ethics and morals come into play. The big question for me is, 'Do I share the extra five dollars with your Uncle Jake or do I keep it all for myself?' "

THAT IS A CLASSIC EXAMPLE OF HORIZONTAL MORALITY! It is the kind of morality gangsters use as well as some business people. It doesn't take very long until such an attitude filters down to members of the whole society.

When it does, it means the destruction of that society. One of our modern prophets stated, "We are literally tearing down all the walls of good behavior and in so doing we are dismantling our society block by block just as effectively as if we were hit by an earthquake. We are in a sad state of affairs."

A Layman To The Rescue

Nehemiah was a layman. A young man born to a people defeated and whose city of Jerusalem was in ruin. Nehemiah was given a job, a real dog of a job. He became cup bearer to the King. This was a high risk position because it was his job to prove that the wine the King drank was not poisoned. As a slave of a defeated people and in such a position of jeopardy, you could hardly expect very much from Nehemiah. Nehemiah surprised everyone simply because he trusted God and he was concerned in living his life responsibly. He felt God expected him to do his very best no matter what life handed him. We have a word that speaks of that attitude, we call it stewardship. Stewardship for Nehemiah wasn't something apart from his daily life. Stewardship to him was a way of life, a lifestyle. Several yers ago I wrote my definition as such, *"Stewardship receives all of life as a gracious gift of God and uses all of life so that everyone is aware of its true source."* That explains Nehemiah to a "T." Even though he never said much to the King about his hopes and dreams for his beloved Jerusalem, yet, his lifestyle of honesty and compassion spoke for him. The King could sense that something was troubling Nehemiah and thus he inquired as to the source of his sadness.

Dreams — Are They God's Dreams?

Again the depth of Nehemiah's faith in God comes to the surface. Like the psalmist, he would not forget his spiritual roots as found in the temple and the city of Jerusalem, which now lay in ruins. Nehemiah desired with all his heart to rebuild the city of God. He had big dreams because they were God inspired dreams. So many people go through life with no dreams and end up with a handful of nightmares of despair. Nehemiah first spoke to God and then he told the King about his desire and dream to rebuild Jerusalem. The King was so impressed with the responsible faith of this young layman he decided to give him a leave of absence and adequate resources to go and rebuild his dream city. He was given official papers to proceed and off he went to Jerusalem. Alas, when he arrived he was shocked to find the city was in total destruction. So great was the destruction that he couldn't even ride his donkey through the streets. He had to go on foot. The situation looked absolutely hopeless, and it was, without God, but Nehemiah had faith in God and His promises. Nehemiah knew that God was the God of creation who delighted in taking chaos and making all things beautiful again. Nehemiah had learned from his faith in God that just when things look like they are five minutes to midnight that in reality they are just five minutes to dawn.

Pray God And Tell The People

It was then that Nehemiah did pray God and let the people know of the plan that God had in store for them. They were now being given the privilege of bringing Glory to God through their response to rebuild Jerusalem.

Hear him as he speaks to them, *"You see the trouble we are in. Jerusalem lies in ruin. Come let us build the walls of Jerusalem that we may no longer suffer disgrace."*

It was then that he revealed to them how the hand of the Lord was upon him and that he had a letter from the King authorizing the work. The contagion of his burning enthusiasm strikes fire in the hearts of the people and with one voice and one heart they cry, "Let us rise and build, so they strengthened their hands for the good work." And the thrilling part of the story is that they did rise and build the entire wall of Jerusalem, more than four miles of it and it was anywhere from twelve feet to twenty feet thick and they did it all in the incredibly short time of fifty-two days. The scriptures give us the secret of their success. *"So we built the wall because the people had a mind to work."*

Your Part In God's Plan

It is fantastic what people working together can do when they are ready to respond to the promptings of the Word of God. It is thrilling to read in the 3rd and 4th chapters of the Book Nehemiah how they dug into the task. Family after family is named, the priests, the sellers of perfume, the goldsmiths, the merchants, *each rose and repaired the wall in front of their own home.* Each played their part. Each assumed their responsibility with zeal. They knew that if one fouled out the whole venture would be in jeopardy. Basically isn't that exactly what God expects of each one of us in the church? There is no excuse for goofing off in the Kingdom of God. It is true you may be only one, but you are one. You can't do everything but you can do something. God didn't put any of us on this earth merely to occupy space and to draw our breath and our salary. He has given everyone some talent and regardless whether they be great or small He isn't interested in the size but in the faithfulness you demonstrate in using His gifts to you to bring praise to His Name and Glory. He is *counting on you to maintain the spiritual front right there where you are in front of your door.* It was remarkable how the people responded to God's call under Nehemiah.

The Fly In The Ointment

Everyone got into the act with only one exception. The scriptures tell how the Tekoites rose and repaired the wall, but some of their Noblemen, their big shots, *"would not put their necks into the work of the Lord."* This is true in every church, a few who want to be counted as church members but who will not be committed to anything. Jesus spoke of people like that. People who hang around the edges but who refuse to whole heartedly enter into the Kingdom. What is worse, by their bad influence and example, they block entrance so others cannot come in. In the case of Nehemiah it was a few bigwigs who fouled out. But when Jesus spoke about this negative attitude, He spoke of the one talent people who, because they can't be big wheels, despise their talent to the point they bury it. Recall how the Mater these upbraided people, *"You rascal . . . throw him out, and give his one talent to someone that will use it."* It is the old story, if you don't use it, you lose it. After all, to God it isn't how much or how little you have been given in time, talent, or money — it's what you do with what you have and how faithful you are in its use. Recall He gave the same commendation to both the five talent man as the two talent man.

"Well done thou good and faithful servant. You have been found faithful with little therefore I will trust you with much. Enter into the joy of your Master."

Substitution — God Always Provides

Even though the Noblemen of the Tekoites fouled out, God would get His work done by other hands. We read that when these few Nobles failed to function, their common people, as if to put their Nobles to shame, rose up and finished their allotted section of the wall and then went on to do another section of the wall beyond the call of duty. Thank God, in every church you can find such blessed souls, God's noble people. You can always spot them for they carry with them some of the fragrance of Mary of Bethany, who counted it a sheer joy to lavish her gifts of love upon her Lord. Of course there are those who will criticize such lavish devotion.

Recall how one, Judas Iscariot, said of Mary's gift, "Why this waste?"

Jesus didn't think it was a waste. In fact He defended her and declared that what she had done was a "beautiful thing" and wherever this Gospel is preached the fragrance of her gift will be remembered. It reminds me of those startling words of St. Paul who reminds us, *"Nothing you ever do for Him is ever lost or wasted."* These words always make me look at my giving to the work of my Lord. *Does it reveal my deep devotion and love for Him? After all I don't give my money to the church, but I support the church because I love my Lord. Therefore my giving is a privilege and I always pray that it might be an act of worship. To me nothing else will do.*

St. Paul again said about giving, *"Don't give it grudgingly or out of necessity."* Such an attitude spoils the gift and can be more harmful than good. Recall Cain's offering. It never got off of the ground, but only led to more hatred against God and his brother.

Really there is only one attitude of giving that is pleasing to the Lord and that is the Attitude of Gratitude. I guess that is why in the church we never talk about *"giving to something"* but rather *"giving from something."* All giving that is pleasing to God is that which is a grateful response to His amazing Grace. We *don't give to get, we give because we have gotten*, everything we own, and have, and are, from God. The common people of the Tekoites had such a spirit. There is testimony that Moses found such a spirit among God's people when he called upon Israel to give of their wealth in order to build the tabernacle in the wilderness. Because the project was an act of worship to God, He insisted that only those of willing heart come and bring their gifts as a thank offering. So overwhelming was the response, that they received more than enough to complete the project. Fact of the matter is that Moses finally had to tell the people to hold back, that they had received more than they could handle. This could happen here at this church *if it is God you are trying to please and bring glory to His name.* It happened also under Nehemiah, and the wall was built "for the people had a mind to work."

Reverse Miracle

We often read about the day when Joshua led the hosts of the Lord round and round the walls of Jericho until the walls came tumbling down, but that isn't nearly as exciting as the miracle of Nehemiah who through God's great spirit was able to build again the walls of the city of Jerusalem. Of course it wasn't easy because we know that evil is never happy at the success of good. Nehemiah had enemies that tried to sabotage his program. Fellows like Sanballot and Tobiah and a host of their tricky friends. Their vandalism got so bad that many of the workers, in an effort to protect themselves, had to work with a sword in one hand and a trowel in the other. When the enemy found that they couldn't stop the work, then they challenged Nehemiah to come on down and fight like a man. How often our old world in its sinfulness challenges us to come down to their level of apathy and corruption. Thanks be to God Nehemiah knew where he was needed and would not let the idle threats side track him from God's plans and will.

As you go forward in your venture for God and you become discouraged at times, remember the words of Nehemiah as he gave answer to Sanballot; *"I cannot come down for I am doing a great work."*

Some years ago when my congregation was entering a massive building venture, I wrote these words to remind each of us of the privilege that is given to "Rise and build to the Glory of God." The article follows:

We The People — Plus

It takes people called of God to build a Church.
All kinds of people . . . rich and poor, small and great,
Yet people fired with a common devotion to Christ.

People . . .

with a burning desire to do all in their power
   to help establish His Kingdom on Earth
      that early — the child — may learn the Father's love
            — the teenager — the path of wisdom
            — the parent — the unity in Christ
            — the aged — the wondrous hope of
               Glory

Therefore to this end . . .

  We the people
    varied in taste and talent
  Unite in Christ . . .
    to rise, to build, that His Kingdom
      might triumph in our day.

CHAPTER 12

Stewardship Ideas

Communications Essential

When I served on the Office of Communication Board of the LCA we had a standing joke that bode us well. It was a story of a woman that appeared before a judge seeking a divorce.

The judge then asked her, "Do you have any grounds?"
"Yes sir, I have three acres," was the reply.
"No, no, I mean do you have a grudge?"
"No, I don't, but I have a carport."
"I'm sorry, but does your husband beat you up?" asked the judge.
"No sir, I always get up before him."
The judge in exasperation asked, "Woman, why do you want a divorce?"
"Well, judge, you see my husband and I seem to have a problem of communication!"

Pray God — Tell The People Now!

I am convinced that so many of our churches are beset by the same problem. The best thing you can do as a pastor is to keep your people informed by any and all means. How many churches foolishly cut out subscriptions to the National Church Magazine in order to save a little money, or cut down on their publication of a weekly church paper? Is it any wonder people lose interest in the church? Being in the dark, they certainly don't feel very much as if they want to support a dark horse. Keep your people informed, and by all means see to it that every copy of your church paper has more than a church calendar of events. I always made it a habit to write a Pastor's Column every week with something inspirational or educational concerning the Church of Christ and His Mission among us.

Following this article I have included a few of the Pastor's Columns I wrote and printed prior to our Loyalty Sunday. Again, the National Church has many fine brochures concerning the work of the church around the world. Send for them, use them, bring them to the attention of your people. Get them excited about becoming participants in the whole church. They will respond and they will enrich the life of the local congregation. One year alone, my congregation in Sheboygan had over seventeen members serving on State and National Boards of the church. We had men, women, and youth filling jobs on the district level. We had one doctor who would go to Africa every year to do eye surgery. We had elected Board Members for the college, and Officers of the Synod. With the help of my congregation, I headed up the whole Lutheran World Relief for the whole state and year after year our people produced *more than 50 percent* of the national output of blankets and quilts. We averaged about 150,000 a year, year after year. Our people were involved because we kept them informed and comissioned them to accept the challenge of "doing all things for the love of Christ." Wow, I get excited just writing about it. People want to be enlisted. They want to give. For the love of God, don't stand in their way. Some years ago I fashioned a stewardship pamphlet for the stewardship program of our Synod. One of them I called, "Your Hand in the Harvest." It was a reminder that Jesus has chosen us, we didn't choose Him. He chose us for a purpose and that purpose is that we might bear fruit and that fruit would remain. What an offer. Our Lord calls us to share in the joy of having our hand in the harvest.

Pastor's Column

I can testify from my own experience how valuable a "Pastor's Column" in the church's newspapers can be. I always worked hard at these little columns because I knew that I would be preaching to fifty or sixty percent of the people who didn't make it to church that Sunday. I often got phone calls and letters from homebound persons and even other pastors thanking me for those tiny bits of inspiration and help. Of course, it meant work, but I can say it was well worth it. I can say with Luther, it proved to be a good external discipline to put the great Gospel news into small packages. Jesus was a master at such things. Look again at His parables. He even used a quip of humor to drive home His message. After all a Christian is so secure in the love of God through Christ that he or she can laugh at some of the absurdities of life. A case in point . . . see the first Pastor's Column I wrote just prior to Thanksgiving. It is silly, but when you finish reading it I know that you will agree that so often we have to lose something before we appreciate just how much we have taken all these blessing for granted.

Pastor's Column

Thanksgiving — Sense And Non-Sense

NONSENSE . . . Perhaps you have heard of the Duke who went duck hunting and the Duke forgot to duck so they had roast Duke for dinner. I thought I would toss off that bit of humor since November can get pretty drab. Recall the quip . . . NO leaves . . . NO grass . . . NO flowers . . . NO vember. It is funny how we have to lose things before we really appreciate them.

Thumb Thanks

I closed a door upon my thumb,
    and now my thumb is sore.
To tie my tie or open a door is quite a chore,
    when your thumb is sore.
And what is more, I never gave thanks,
    for my thumb before.
I just used my thumb and took it for granted,
    forevermore.
My thankfulness I had kept in store,
    until my thumb got sore.
"Thumb Thanks . . . Forgive me Lord"

Note: In 1967 I had written a Thanksgiving Sermon in which I urged my people to remember to say "Thank You" to those who touched their lives. It was then I realized that maybe I ought to practice what I preach. It dawned on me that I never officially thanked my congregation for all they meant to me. I got busy and composed the following and sent a copy to each member. It brought a magnificent response from the people. I made it a point to send a Thanksgiving letter to our people every year. Let me share it with you.

Miracle Letter

Dear Members of First Church:

As we enter into the Thanksgiving Season, I want you to know that I thank God always for you and your loyal-hearted love. I wish that I had the time to drop into your home this coming week and shake your hand and say, "Thank you."

At this season of the year I am mindful of the great host of teachers and officers doing such a wonderful job planting the seeds of the Gospel in the hearts of our many children through Parish Education. I think also of the many youth organizations and dedicated service that goes into making them a success.

I think of the Church Council and the host of subcommittees that carry on the administrative work of the congregation. Such jobs make for much work and much criticism. I think of the Lutheran Church Women keeping the heart of the congregation alive and tender to the needs of others. They minister with lessons, prayers, and needles through Lutheran World Relief, Lutheran Social Services, Cancer Dressing Group, Keepie Keep, and Altar Guild. I am mindful for the Couples Club Yo-Ho and Morning Star and the fine Adult Classes that play an essential part of the life of our church. Of course there is the inspiration and beauty that enhances our worship through organ and choirs. How grateful I am for all these wonderful people who serve with such devotion.

But I would also like to say "Thank You" to you, Mr., Mrs., or Ms. Church Goer. Your regular attendance at services and at Communion is a real witness of God's love in your life. I am grateful too, that you stand ready to prove the reality of your Faith by your generous giving not only to the local congregation but to the support of the work of the whole church.

While I thank God for you, let me say "Thank You to You." May God continue to bless you.

Gratefully yours in Christ,
Pastor G. Wm. Genszler

Pastor's Column

Let's Talk About Money

Many people are frustrated because they feel that their job is a bore and a waste of time. A person can only be productive and happy in their work when they feel that their job fulfills a satisfying use of their time and talents. This is of prime importance. However, there will come a time, even when a person has found the work they wish to do, when they will say to their employer, "Fine, I like the job. Now please talk to me about money." THAT IS ONLY GOOD COMMON SENSE.

Matrimony And Money

Nothing can ever take the place of LOVE in courtship and marriage. To marry for any other reason will set the stage for matrimonial suicide. Love means the total unrestricted gift of ones whole self to the other.

When a couple finally agree to be thus committed to each other in Holy Matrimony, there comes the time when they must sit down together and say, "because we love each other, now please let us talk of money. THAT IS ONLY GOOD COMMON SENSE.

Christians And Cash

Everyone will agree that to be a Christian means to be totally committed to Christ in body, mind, and soul. Anything less than such a commitment is sheer hypocrisy. It is simply because we love Him and trust Him, that we feel that there must come a time when we ought to discuss quite candidly our financial support of His church, the Bride of Christ.

Yet when the church suggests such a plan, there are those who cry, "Don't talk to me about money." "We want to know, "Why Not?"

DOESN'T CHRIST DESERVE SOME GOOD COMMON SENSE TOO?

Money talks, pray God our money may speak of our love of Christ.

Pastor's Column

Look Whose Talking

DON'T YOU DESPISE PASTORS AND PRIESTS WHO . . .
    Don't practice what they preach.
    Don't preach what they believe.
    Don't trust what they know to be true.

YOU HAVE A RIGHT TO CRITICIZE SUCH PEOPLE . . .
    They are false prophets. They are cowardly priests.
    They are hypocritical ministers.

THEY PREACH . . . "I BELIEVE IN GOD . . .
    The Father, Almighty . . . and Jesus, his Son, Our Lord, and in the Holy Spirit, the Giver of Life."

YET THEY PRACTICE AND LIVE . . .
    As if God didn't exist . . . they are afraid to share.
    They worry themselves sick.

THEY KNOW THAT JESUS IS GOD . . .
    Yet they follow not His command, they share not His love.
    They deny Him as Lord.

THEY KNOW THAT GOD CAN PROVIDE ALL THINGS . . .
    Yet they can't afford to be generous. Tithing is outlandish.
    How can they manage.

DON'T YOU DESPISE PRIESTS WHO . . .
    Don't practice what they preach.
    Preach what they don't believe.
    Don't trust that which they know is true.

HAS IT EVER DAWNED ON YOU THAT WE ARE PRIESTS OF GOD?

The Bible says of all believers, "You are priests of God; (1 Peter 2:9)

"You are priests of God," says Revelation 1, 6:5-10

THE QUESTION COMES HOME . . . DO YOU AND I
    Practice what we preach
    Preach what we believe
    Trust Him who is the Truth?
"Lord be merciful to me a sinner"

Pastor's Column

Thought After Thought

Whenever I think of the Incarnation or when I come to the Lord's Table, I think of an old Communion Hymn that begins with the words, "draw nigh and take the Body of our Lord." There is one particular stanza that speaks of receiving, "the pledges of salvation here." The Christ of the Manger and the Christ of the Sacrament are mine today because God PLEDGED to send His only begotten Son to be our Savior. On Calvary He paid that pledge in full. That took some kind of deep commitment. We are called to share in that committed life of God.

Church Membership Means "You're In"

When we joined the church we pledged to be found faithful to the Lord Jesus Christ and all that He stands for.

When asked, we answered, "Yes, by the help of God."

I am sure that most of us meant it. At least, that is the way it started out. Then came the test.

"Would you willingly like to pledge to support the work of your Lord each week?"

Unfortunately some say, "Well, I am afraid that I can't pledge, but I will try to give."

These are just a few of the annual excuses used to try to back out of any solid commitment to support the work or our Lord.

No Place To Hide

Jesus was well acquainted with the human attempt to wiggle out of our responsibility (a good word indicating our RESPONSE to His AMAZING GRACE). Jesus spoke of those who "with one accord make excuse." He made it clear that excuses just don't excuse, they only cheat the person out of the joy of being committed to Him, "who loves and gave Himself for us."

Let's set the record straight. True, we don't know what's coming tomorrow, but we do know WHO is coming tomorrow or the next day or the next day after that. Life is full of uncertainties for everyone. One thing for sure, you have Christ, and He is no uncertainty. Certainly we ought to be able to trust Him to provide all things needful. He's been doing it for years. Frankly, He promises to be there forever for you. It must hurt Him terribly to hear us say, "Really, I can't muster enough faith in Him to make a committed pledge to His Work."

"Oh Lord, increase my faith." AMEN.

Pastor's Column

Me And My Money

Our Stewardship Committee got into a lengthy discussion on the matter of tithing.

Long ago God's word declared, "The tithe is mine, saith the Lord."

God never left us in the dark as to the way He would finance His church. The problems arise from the fact that too many people do not go along with this kind of thinking. We find it difficult for us to actually try His way. The Committee assigned one of the members to come up with all the reasons why most people find it impossible to tithe. Our poet laureate, Peg Nemeth dashed off this clever little poem that touches the real root of the problem.

Ten Percent Of Zero Is Zero

To give ten percent is really too much!
   I haven't enough coming in
      The goverment takes far more than its share
      And that is where the trouble begins

Lord, look at my bills, food, heating and light
      The price tag on clothing's a sin
         My auto consumes so very much gas
         Sometimes I just want to give in

TITHING . . . forget it
   There's simply no way
      The high cost of living is no joke
         I'm sure that there are others
           Who earn more than I do
              Please don't ask me just now cause I'm broke

Leftovers That Leave You Out

So often we forget the main purpose of the tithe. The tithe is to be given first before you blow the whole check. It is a grateful recognition that for you and all that you have, God comes first. He does — You know! Without Him you wouldn't have anything. He even gives you the ability to make money. To ignore that source of blessing is like killing the goose that laid the golden egg. Tithing is the simplest way of keeping God foremost in your life. With Him, for starters, you will never be broke again. When you have Him first, you will always have adequate resources available to you.

God's promise concerning tithing is written in Malachi 3:10, *"Bring the full tithes into the storehouse, that there may be food in my house, and thereby put me to the tests, says the Lord of Hosts, if I will not open the windows of heaven for you and pour down for you an overflowing of blessing."*

Pastor's Column

Time To Unmask (Advent)

It is midnight in the church. The last hour of the old church year is history. The masquerade is over and it is time to take off the mask. Advent Repentance is time to look honestly at ourselves as we really are and not according to facades we have constructed. It is time to look at ourselves according to the one standard God declares as the measure of our Faith-namely, HAVE WE BEEN FAITHFUL. This requires a good bit of LOYALTY to Him on our part.

Loyalty To Whom

Our age has been betrayed again and again by misplaced loyalty. Politicians will betray people to remain loyal to their political group. People in business often are so loyal to their company that they will let pollution continue or false profits exist. Many people are so loyal to profits that they will sacrifice their principles. Is there a way to check our loyalties?

Jesus once said, *"Where your treasure is, there your heart will be also."* Would anyone be able to guess that we have been loyal to God by looking over the stubs in our checkbook or by the checkmarks on our communion records? These may be very small things indeed, but they are indications of our inner loyalties. St. Paul went so far as to say, *"Moreover your very giving proves the reality of your FAITHFULNESS."* The new church year at Advent time is a season that calls us to renew our loyalty to the Christ who proved His loyalty to us from a Cross.

18 Years Tall (A letter from a young member)

"This is my church. It is composed of people like me. We make it what it is. I want it to be a church that is a light on the paths of pilgrims, leading them to goodness, truth, and beauty. It will be, if I am. It will be friendly, if I am. Its pews will be filled if I help to fill them. It will bring other people into its worship and fellowship if I bring them. It will be a church of loyalty and love, of fearlessness and faith, if I, who make it what it is, am filled with these qualities. Therefore, I dedicate myself to the task of being what I want my church to be."

Pastor's Column

Dreaming Of A White Christmas

Just ten days to shop until Christmas is here,
    So buy all your gifts for the ones you hold dear,
And wrap them up lovely regardless of cost
    Your gifts show your love not your profit or loss.

Rich gifts you must buy to please all your kin,
    And mortgage your future their favor to win.
You treat them, each one, with birthday delight.
    With gifts under tree as you sing "Silent Night."
And then as you sing you remember — too late,
    You've gifts for them all — but Lord Jesus must wait.
How soon we forget what THIS DAY really is,
    For Christmas speaks birthday — the birthday that's His.

Some sing of Christmas both snowy and white,
    "Our Father, please help us to dream Christmas RIGHT.
O give us clear vision, not sleepy-eyed mist,
    To make Baby Jesus the HEAD OF OUR LIST.

THIS SUNDAY IS LOYALTY SUNDAY

PLAN NOW TO COME TO CHURCH TO WORSHIP

PLAN NOW TO PICK UP YOUR NEW CHURCH ENVELOPES

PLAN NOW TO LET YOUR PLEDGE FOR THE COMING YEAR SHOW THAT CHRIST HEADS YOUR LIST, NOW AND THROUGH THE YEAR.

CHAPTER 13
Show And Tell

Let Your Light So Shine Before All People

So many times we get the idea that our giving is a very private matter and thus we hide our light under a bushel. I'm not sure this is the best policy. Jesus went out of his way to help His disciples witness the giving of others in the Temple, to teach them how our giving gives witness to our love of God. He praised the generosity of the rich people but He was absolutely overjoyed with the gift of the widow who had given all.

Hidden Light

I believe my father made a mistake when he kept secret his giving to the church. It wasn't until after he died that the congregation learned that their pastor was one of the largest givers in that congregation. Faithfully he had contributed a dollar a day, $365 a year out of a $2,400 a year salary. My father had often preached sermons on tithing and giving, but to most people that was simply preachers talk. Many people didn't know that the preacher gave any money to the church since he was the pastor. My father always practiced what he preached but not many people knew about his love of God, expressed in his worshipful giving.

Not Proud Or Ashamed To Tell

I often have told my congregations about our introduction into the joy of tithing. In my first parish my salary was $113.00 a month and I had to rent a two room apartment out of that sum for $10 a week. If we were to tithe it would mean 10 percent of $27 a week. Since I had always preached that tithing was a reasonable first step to Christian giving, we decided to trust God and we pledged $3 a week. I can honestly say it was one of the wisest things we ever did. Setting that money aside first always focused our minds on the goodness of God and we were more than blessed.

Tell It Like It Is

I told my congregation in Sheyboygan about our venture in faith through tithing. I encouraged my people to give it a try and discover for themselves the joy. Evidently my words stirred some young hearts. I had a pathologist in my congregation who often would discuss the content of my sermons with his children at the Sunday dinner table. On Loyalty Sunday I gave a strong sermon on tithing. Naturally the conversation at the doctor's dinner table turned to the subject of tithing.

One of his sons spoke up and asked, "Dad, our family tithes doesn't it? I noticed that you always put a $20 bill in your envelope. That is a tithe, isn't it?"

Dr. Jim was slow in making an answer.

"I am afraid our giving doesn't qualify as a tithe."

Quickly, one of the other children spoke up and asked, "Gee Dad, what would a tithe be for us?"

Dr. Jim told me he swallowed hard at this juncture. He knew he was trapped because the kids would press him for the truth. Slowly he took out his ballpoint and began to write numbers on a paper napkin to figure out just what a tithe would amount to. After he had it all figured out, he didn't want the kids to see the results so he crumbled up the napkin. The oldest daughter grabbed the napkin and flattened it to see the results.

"Wow, $107 a week," she cried.

"Holy Cow, Dad, you mean to say that you make that much money?" (*Please remember this was back in the early '60s, when $50,000.00 was a fortune.*)

New Vision Through The Tithe

Dr. Jim and his family decided right then and there to tithe. As he told the whole congregation in a temple talk, *it wasn't until they decided to tithe and he saw just how much a tithe would be, that they realized just how generous God had been to them. It helped them realize that God had long ago opened the windows of heaven and blessed them over abundantly year after year.* It wasn't until they began to tithe that they had their eyes opened to the magnificence of God's bounty. Up until then "they had been blind, but now they see." Our very giving can be a real, "show and tell time," giving evidence to all, *that we do love and trust God above all things.*

CHAPTER 14
Appeals Not Appalling

What About Special Appeals

I recall many years ago when our National Church had so many different special emphasis Sundays that one pastor wrote in asking for the following resolution:

"RESOLVE, that we set aside at least one Sunday a month when we can emphasize and preach the GOSPEL."

There is no doubt about it, the church does have a great host of very important items that need support and attention. I know that there are some experts who feel that "Special appeals" have a way of cutting into the regular support of the local congregation. This can happen, however, I found that this need not be the case. I learned early that a plan can be established that will give your people a chance to support many of these appeals according to their varied interests and their varied interests are in direct proportion to their knowledge of where their money is going and what it is accomplishing.

Accomplished Giving

Every year I had the Church Council and the Finance Committee study just which appeals we felt were most important and then we presented the list to the congregation for approval. We then designate a special item to a particular month and announced that the Communion Offerings that month were going to support that item (unless otherwise designated). Usually I made it a point to highlight the work of that agency or program in the Church Paper and in the Sunday Bulletin. Our List:

January	— World Mission
February	— Seminary
March	— World Hunger
April	— Local Assistance Fund, Food Pantry
May	— Lutheran World Relief
June	— Youth & Scholarship Fund
July	— Lutheran Home for Aged
August	— World Hunger
September	— College Support Fund
October	— Lutheran Social Services
November	— Lutheran World Relief
December	— Local Assistance (HOFF)

People Will Respond

I have always been amazed with the wonderful way people responded to the items listed because they had a hand in approving the list. Let's face it, everyone has some special interest and when they are given the opportunity they will support it generously. For example, our Youth and Scholarship Fund always had plenty of money to send scores of young people to camp and to Youth Convention because we had many people who did not have children of their own and they wanted to help. Our Local Assistance Fund called HOFF (Household of Faith Fund) was a discretionary fund to assist families in need with food, rent, fuel. It also sent plants to our shut-ins a week before Easter and Christmas (not leftover from the services). This was a gift to say we cared to send the best. We also sent gift certificates to the Staff of the Synodical Office to let them know that we appreciated their efforts on our behalf. I did everything I could to teach our congregation to be thoughtful of others and generous. This generosity spilled over into support of the current fund as well. So often pastor's will preach, "It is more blessed to give than to receive," and again, "Give and it will be given unto you" and then fail to follow through. It doesn't take the congregation very long to see through this pastor who can only seek to keep all the money at home. That pastor will soon lose his or her credibility. They teach by their example that begging is more important to them than teaching the joys of unselfish stewardship.

Please Remember

Please remember that your people are being approached on every side to help support this worthy cause or that worthy project. REMEMBER many of our church people are giving great sums of money to answer these appeals BECAUSE THEY ARE NOT AWARE THAT THEIR OWN CHURCH IS ALREADY DOING THE SAME KIND OF HELP AND IN MANY CASES DOING IT BETTER AND MORE EFFICIENTLY.

A case in point. When TV brought to our attention the famine in Ethiopia, there was an overwhelming response and much of it came from church members. Many were not aware that Lutheran World Relief was already there with tons of relief assistance. The other thing that many people didn't realize was that the church was doing all of this wonderful work with less than 5 percent being spent on publicity and administration. Again when several secular organizations called for money to dig wells in India, our own Lutheran World Relief had already dug more than 4,000 wells and made many communities self supporting because of the water we helped provide.

Pastors, pray God. Then get yourself informed about what your church is doing and then tell the people and they will amaze you with their generosity. Believe me, I have found that the more generous my people are with others, the more generous they are at home. Generosity has become for them a "new lifestyle."

CHAPTER 15
Fund Raisers

Extra-Ordinary Measures

Anyone who knows me is aware of the fact that I am a firm believer in training all of our members to support the church for no other reason than they love their Lord. This should make all of our giving a joyful act of worship. In another chapter, I have dealt with the many ways I have found to teach these lessons in GRACE GIVING. I am a firm believer in encouraging my people to come into the House of the Lord and there as an act of worship make their commitment to the support of both the current and benevolence programs of the church. The only constraint they face is the Love of Christ and their response to Him. It works. I have forty-two years and four parishes to testify to the beauty of such an approach.

But what about capitol funding for buildings? There, I must say, we are in a different "ball game." I have used professional fund programs both commercial and church (LLM). In most instances they have been most helpful in raising the sights of our members to greater giving. From my experience I have found the value of such professional fund raisers is the person who comes to direct the program. I have had both good and bad. Fortunately for me, the first one to come from the Wells Corporation was a retired Methodist pastor who was dedicated to His Lord. He very carefully laid out the spiritual context for all of our giving. He never let us forget the motivation of our acts.

I must say as I watched him work I thought of the scene from Hamlet when he had some roving actors give him a demonstration of their acting ability. They do a bit of Greek Tragedy with such conviction that even Hamlet is really touched by it. Then it dawns on Hamlet that if these players, here in make believe, can cause such a stir; how much more should he be moved to act. After all, the actors only had a *case*, but Hamlet had a *cause*. He was the son of a dear father murdered.

As I listened to the Fund Counselor, I felt, if they can cause such a stir to lift the congregational giving, how much more should I, a pastor of the Gospel with the news of a God who died and rose for us, be aflame with the message. The Fund Raiser had the technical knowledge to perform it, but as a Christian, I had the dynamics to fearlessly proclaim it.

I shall never forget the honest confession of the pastor from Wells when he said, "Bill, if our pastors would only realize what power they have in the words of scripture and would use them regularly, not as law, but as joyful response to the God's wondrous Grace, they would put every Fund Counselor out of business. And he was right, but unfortunately I find too many pastors are not convinced in their own giving and thus soft pedal the message.

I suppose one of the advantages of a professional Fund Raiser comes from the fact that you have to pay them. We are a funny people. Usually if we don't pay for something, we don't listen to it.

Let me give you a humorous experience I had in my first parish in the Badlands of North Dakota.

Cash On The Barrel Head

Every year the neighboring high schools would call on me to give their Commencement address. After a while it got a little much and the interesting thing about it was that seldom did I even get a note of thanks for doing it. I learned from a lawyer in Fargo that he always charges $100 for such events.

When he learned that I was doing this for nothing, he told me I was crazy. I decided that I had enough of this, so I planned to turn down all these offers to speak gratis at high schools in neighboring towns.

Then one day a letter came from a place called Halliday. They asked me to speak. This time they had added a p.s. They wanted to know what my fee was for speaking. Here was my chance to get out of this thankless job. I wrote back and told them my fee was $25 (and that was a lot of money back when my salary was only $113 a month). I thought such a fee might free up some of my effort and time. I was pleasantly surprised by receiving invitations from three other schools asking me if I would come to their schools for the same fee I was receiving from Halliday School.

My point is, I guess if you have to pay for something, you will think it is important enough to listen to it and follow through.

I must admit that there are some phases of Funding Drives that I am not too keen about. I find that they would be unnecessary if our people were totally committed Christians. I am still trying to find such a congregation. If I did, I'm not sure they would let me in.

I had one member of my congregation become a very effective Fund Councilor for the Lutheran Layman's Movement for Stewardship. He could speak from the heart about the joy of Christian giving and talk about the blessings found in tithing even when for a time the company he worked for discontinued many jobs, including his. He wasn't play acting by doing scenes from Hamlet, but his was the testimony of a heart on fire for God. He could speak from the heart because he had a cause and that cause was Christ.

If you are planning to use an outside source for a Capital Fund Campaign, be sure to meet and study, not only their methods but their motivation behind their efforts. I have always tried to live by the slogan, "Never let your dynamics suffer at the hands of your technicalities."

CHAPTER 16
Com"Mission" Or Volunteer

You, You, And You!

My brother-in-law was a Marine in the Second World War and he distinguished himself as the photographer who took the pictures of the Japanese Fleet in the harbor at Truk Island. Twenty-two Marines secretly flew in and gave our command the knowledge of where to send our bombers to destroy a good number of Japanese ships. Naturally, these men were considered heroes and were decorated appropriately.

I shall never forget when my wife first met her brother, Albert, after he got home.

"Golly, Albert," she said, "You certainly were brave to volunteer for such a dangerous mission."

Albert replied, "Look Dorothy, you are not acquainted with Marine procedure. They simply line you up and then say, 'we need twenty-two volunteers, you, you, you, etc, . . . get on the plane.' "

The little exchange of words got me to thinking about the way my Lord recruited His disciples. I suppose some of them thought that they had volunteered to follow Him, but He set the record straight.

He reminded them, *"You did not choose me, I chose you, and I chose you for a purpose; that you might bear fruit and that that fruit might remain."*

Again and again Jesus didn't call for volunteers, but He commissioned and appointed people to do certain things. Even His transportation bore that mark.

Recall his words, *"Just tell them that the Lord has need of it."*

I often think we make a mistake in the church asking for volunteers. I agree that volunteers are needed in the community to take meals on wheels, or work for the United Way. I think the church is somehow different. Let me see if I can give you an illustration from my experience.

When I accepted the "call" to be the pastor of my third congregation, I was told that they had a difficult job in getting enough ushers in spite of the fact that they asked for volunteers time and time again.

One of the problems of asking for volunteers in the church is that it appears that the job isn't very important and who wants to commit themselves to something lacking in importance?

I asked the Church Council to sit down with me and go through the Church Directory and put down the name of anyone they felt could usher if they wanted to usher. The group came up with a list of eighty-five names. We then composed a letter which we sent to each one of these men. The substance of the letter ran something like this:

> Dear George:
>   The church Council and pastor, after prayerful consideration have chosen you to become an usher for our congregation. As a committed Christian we feel that you will be more than willing to serve your church and your Lord in this very special and important work.
>   According to the new ushering schedule, each usher will serve one Sunday every other month. (Six times a year) Since you usually attend the early service, we will assign you to that time slot. The Captain for your team will contact you for the instruction sessions. We know that you will enjoy being a vital part of the worship of Our Lord.
>   If you find it impossible to serve, please contact the pastor.

There was a lot more information in the letter, but I think you get the idea. I was happy to report that we only had three turndowns. I am convinced that every job in the Lord's church is an opportunity to serve Him, and when I ask someone to fill a position or do a job I feel that it is a privilege afforded them and not just a dreary duty.

Reverse English

I have found that so many pastors go about acquiring help in such a negative way. They remind me of a friend of mine who was asked to call up his sister and offer to take her for a nice ride. My friend wasn't too keen about the idea, but dutifully he called his sister.

"Hello," he said, "Helen, you don't want to go for a ride, do you?"

What could the poor woman say!

It is interesting to note that the word "commission" is made up of the word "com," from the Latin meaning "with" and the rest of the word is "mission." Every baptized Christian brought into the family of God is automatically "with mission" and the mission is terribly important because it comes from the Lord. It always thrills me when I remember what St. Paul said, *"Nothing we ever do for Christ is ever lost or wasted."*

In the light of such thinking I never hesitate to engage people in the work of the Lord. The "mission," if they choose to accept it, can be a mighty blessing in disguise. Ask Simon of Cyrene. He learned the everlasting joy of life's enriching compulsions. I have letters of gratitude from many people who have discovered the same. Let the world seek its volunteers to do its blessed work among the people, but let the redeemed of the Lord rejoice with St. Paul, when he said, *"It is not only my privilege to believe in Jesus Christ, but also to work and suffer for His sake."* God commissioned His only begotten Son. Can we expect anything less?

CHAPTER 17
Dis — Interested

It Sounds So Logical

It happens in almost every congregation after a few years following a building program. Some genius will compute the amount of money the congregation could save on interest if they had another campaign to wipe out the debt. It sounds so logical, but there is a tremendous price to pay for such action. I have seen its effects. The last parish I have come to serve had indeed paid off its indebtedness far in advance, but because they did, they cut their benevolence giving in half. They never equipped their new building properly. This 2,400 member congregation had one secretary, with one old typewriter and an old mimeograph machine. They had two full time paid staff who were both underpaid. They desperately needed an elevator to make their large basement available for practical use. The church school had very little educational equipment, yet they had paid off their mortgage.

In my third parish, we had the same request by a few Council persons to hurry up and pay off the debt. I was against it and gave my reasons for the same. It was the then former Superintendent of our School Sunday who came to my rescue with a testimony from her own experience. She told us how she and her husband had purchased a home and set it up on a twenty-year mortgage which they could afford. She confessed that she often tried to get her husband to speed up the payments in order to save some interest.

Her husband told her that they had a comfortable mortgage which they could handle. However, the education of their children was far more important than the dumb payments on a house. She agreed that he was very wise in making that statement. They followed his suggestion and the proof of his wisdom was in the fine education they were able to provide for their boys, who both distinguished themselves in very important positions in the world today.

Following her testimony, one of the members of the group asked the question whether we thought the new members joining the church would willingly want to pay toward the mortgage.

It was then one of our new members spoke up and said, "Of course we will. In part, it was the wonderful new facility that attracted us to join and it is only fair that each new generation should have a hand in paying for these benefits."

Too Much Interest In Interest

No one enjoys making interest payments but one thing should always be taken into consideration. The new building, made possible because of a mortgage with interest, will certainly help the congregation to grow. With the increase of membership the congregation will be able to liquidate the indebtedness without slacking off on the staff, programs or missions. People who always want to race through a mortgage in order to save interest often forget why they built the building in the first place.

They remind me of the riverboat captain who got in a race up the Mississippi with another boat. He discovered that he could create more steam power if he burned some of the fat meat from his cargo. It is true he won the race, but at what cost. When he got to the finish line he was first, but he had no cargo to deliver. I like to think of our mortgage payments as our rent for the use of a wonderful facility. "Interesting, to say the least."

CHAPTER 18

Risky Business

I have always delighted in the silly story that I first heard with regard to the risk of Faith.

It seemed that it was one of those old style churches where the balcony was exceedingly steep and it encircled the nave. It was here that the choir was located. One Sunday, a spellbinder of a pastor preached from the pulpit and he was most dramatic. Everyone listened with rapt attention. Members of the choir slid forward in their seats in the balcony and right at a high point of excitement in the sermon, a young choir member fell out of the front row of the balcony. Fortunately her robes got caught in the chandelier. Here she was dangling in mid-air.

The pastor saw her situation and in order to protect her modesty he shouted out, "If anyone looks up, the Lord will strike you blind."

The old codger in the back row whispered to his partner, "I think I'll risk one eye."

Say what you will, the old fellow had a bit of daring. The tragedy of so many church people is that they are afraid to risk even one eye and look up unto the Lord and venture forth in faith wherever he will lead the way.

Dr. Hugh George Anderson On The Risk Of Faith

Some years ago while serving as the Chairman of the Synodical Stewardship Committee, we had opportunity to invite

Dr. Hugh George Anderson, then President of Southern Seminary and now President of Luther College, to come and present a paper on the subject matter "Stewardship as a Life Style." That paper has been reproduced several times, but it was the closing paragraphs that brought into focus the need for the daring risk factor particularly when it comes to money. I have Dr. Anderson's permission to share it with you.

Meanwhile, Back At The Cash Register

Now let's come back to money. I'd like to link it with the other crisis of our times — the crisis of faith. We have often linked faith and money in our talk about stewardship, and usually in that order. The faithful Christian is the contributing Christian. If you believe, then you give. I'd like to suggest that reversing the order might also prove workable.

The basic problem of faith today is the question of God's existence, or more precisely, whether God "makes a difference" in our life or the world. The reason it's so hard to find the answer to that question is that we do everything in our power to make sure that God won't *have* to make a difference. We guard against every unforeseen occurrence; we minimize the variables; we insure ourselves against every possible accident, including "acts of God." In short, we try to put our life on such a secure and self-guaranteed basis that there is no room for any will other than our own. It's as though we set out to discover life in a laboratory that we had tried our best to sterilize. No wonder it is difficult to discover the "mighty acts of God."

Our chief instrument in this attempt to conquer the future is our money. We spend it on insurance, market forecasts, research and development, and even on fortune-tellers. Why not see if this remarkable tool could not be put to another use? Why not set out deliberately to use it as a means of providing the sort of conditions under which God's power *would* become manifest and his presence made known? To carry through our laboratory analogy, I am suggesting that we use money to establish a "culture medium" in which the acts of God may grow and become visible. Now to some details.

Tithing For Fun And Profit

If money is our chief defense against the unforeseen, then one way to allow the unforeseen to happen is to let down our guard — to spend our money in other ways. The tithe has long been debated among Lutherans because it smacked of legalism. Let's forget that; we can never give enough to God. But what about seeing the tithe as a challenge to take a financial risk? What if the purpose of the tithe is not to satisfy God but to make men a little hungry? What if stretching the budget to give a significant portion to God would force us to rely on Him to see us through? I believe two results are guaranteed.

The first result is that God *will* see us through and we will discover that he *does* make a difference. I have known many families who have been challenged to give sacrificially — usually to a building campaign — and who have discovered that the risk they took brought exciting discoveries. There was still enough food for the table; the family focused on their newfound burden and thus learned to share; the "financial crisis" never developed. In other words, by using money to *create* risk rather than to avoid it, a "space" was opened for the graceful touch of God. New friends, new tasks, new joys, and new values crowded onto the scene. It was like a fresh start.

The second result springs from the fact that "where your treasure is, there is your heart also." When a family gives sacrificially to a project — and let's hope that it won't always be a building — they are interested in what happens to their money. When the contribution goes toward a project involving people, the family can see how their small gift is multiplied in its usefulness. Perhaps they also will get involved in the project. Once again the stage is set for God's action. The donor is sensitive to what great things can still be accomplished by money that is given wrapped in love.

Having Everything, Possessing Nothing

There is no better way for faith to grow than to be exposed to the radiation of God's activity in our own lives and the lives of others. A program of financial risk will provide the opening for this radiation to flood upon us. One of the best prospects about the current financial crisis which confronts the church is that it will force us to rely again on the power of God — rather than the interest rate — to multiply our loaves and fishes. Perhaps we are on the brink of a new era of faith in the church, since doubt is a disease of the affluent. To live one's life as a steward is to have all things and possess nothing — a difficult lifestyle, but one that offers alternatives to the most vexing problems of our generation.

CHAPTER 19
Ecumenism — Opportunity Unlimited

A Ding-A-Ling

One of the thrills of my fifty years in the ministry has been the ecumenical exchange that has been taking place, especially since Vatican II.

Someone once defined Ecumenism as "a Roman Catholic drinking Mogen David wine out of a mason jar on Reformation Day." Fortunately, it is something far different. Things have changed for the better. I know something of those days when competition ran rampant and each denomination tried to out do the other. A classic story that I am sure you might enjoy goes like this.

In a small town where the Presbyterians were the biggest and richest church in town, they decided to send to Scotland to purchase a magnificent bell. A bell that would say something about their particular faith. They got the bell. It was a beauty and the first Sunday it rang, it boomed out in deep tones, "Pre — des — tin — a — tion, pre — des — tin — a — tion." It spoke their favorite doctrine.

The Baptists in the town didn't want to be out done, so they too got a bell. Since they couldn't afford a big bell, they got a small bell but it too was to signal forth something concerning their doctrine of Total Immersion. The bell came and on Sunday it rang out in high tones, "be dipped, or be damned, be dipped, or be damned."

Well, the old German Lutheran down the street didn't want to be left out, but they were "tighter than the bark on a tree." So when Sunday came they sent their sexton out with a small hand bell which he rang while vigorously shouting, "pretzels and beer, pretzels and beer."

Fresh Air

Of course we all recognize this as a preposterous story, but it isn't nearly as preposterous as the intolerance that existed between various denominations of the Christian Church. I recall back in the 1920s when my best friend, a Roman Catholic boy had to go to confession and confess that he had sinned by playing with a Lutheran Minister's son.

Of course all of that feeling changed during the Vatican II days. I can recall with joy when Father Cook of the Marquette Theological Department met with two hundred Lutheran Ministers in Minneapolis in a Lutheran church. We were surprised to see him in our church, but we became even more delighted when he said, "I bring you greetings from Rome and I am happy to announce that you are no longer looked upon as "heretics." We now consider you as "separated brothers" in Christ."

The second announcement he made was even more startling. "Our theologians in Rome, after renewed study of the works of Martin Luther, realized that he had much that was right and good and the big mistake Rome made was to drive Luther out of the church. We should have kept him in the church and listened to him. This we are doing today. Pope John the Twenty-third really had opened up the windows of Rome and fresh air is flowing through."

Great Balls Of Fire Lutheran Church

With the new ecumenical attitude on the scene, we found a joy in sharing our great many likenesses rather than our differences. It was great having several Roman Catholic Priests as special friends. One even had me preach his installation sermon in a new parish; several Roman Catholic districts ask permission to print some of my articles and poems in their church papers. The United Church of Canada had me do a five-day workshop on Stewardship. The National Council of Churches asked me to make a presentation on the Stewardship of Loyalty Sunday pledging. My congregation soon followed my lead and they too became very active in ecumenical affairs. They spearheaded the Laubach Literacy Program for the community and the Immigration Refugee Program. They always sent flowers to every church in town when they celebrated an anniversary or a building dedication. When other clergy were in the hospital, we sent flowers and our prayers. It wasn't long until the church had a wonderful reputation for sharing their love in all directions. One Synodical Staff member labeled First United Lutheran Church of Sheboygan as "Great Balls of Fire Lutheran Church," and he was correct. Our people were aflame with the love of Christ and it set other hearts afire as well.

I always encouraged our people to get active in State and County Council of Churches, as well as the District and Synodical programs. It seems the more our people gave of themselves, the more they had to give at home as well. The divine mathematics still is at work and it is in giving that you receive; not that your purpose in giving is to get, no way! But it comes as a wonderful serendipity and that is His surprise for you.

Catholic Cheese And Lutheran Prayers

I must tell you a true experience that I had in 1957. Since I was the State Chairman for Lutheran World Relief, I received a call from the New York Office to go up to Green Bay, Wisconsin to help dedicate a boatload of government cheese bound for Yugoslavia. I would be joined by the Reverend Werner Kuntz of the Board of World Relief for the Missouri Synod. When we arrived we discovered that our boat couldn't be loaded until the next day because a similar boat was being loaded with cheese by the National Catholic Welfare Conference destined for Spain. What to do? Well at the suggestion of the captains of the two ships, we decided that we could hold our dedication service aboard the ship going to Spain. No one would be the wiser. So we went ahead. We thought everything went well. It wasn't until the next day that the Milwaukee Journal came out with big headlines, "LUTHERAN MINISTERS BLESS CATHOLIC CHEESE." The article went on to tell about the Catholic cheese going to Spain on the Tronstad and then they wondered if it should sink on the way to Spain, would they blame it on the "Lutheran prayers?"

We all had a great laugh out of this experience, but what is even more thrilling is the way Catholic World Relief and Church World Service and Lutheran World Relief work so closely together and together we are able to multiply God's mercy to his hurting people around the world.

In Conclusion

Johnnie Come Lately

There is a legend about the train that ran from Mandan, North Dakota to Killdeer, which was at the end of the line. They call it "The Goose." It was a combination of engine, baggage car and passenger section all in one. It was always late in arriving at Killdeer. However, one day it arrived exactly on time.

Many of the local people couldn't believe it happened and so they called up the station to talk to Pete, the station manager.

"Congratulations Pete, this is the first time the train has ever been on time."

Pete laughingly replied, "What do you mean, ON TIME, this is yesterday's train."

A sequel to this legend is the day that a woman called up the station to ask if the train for that day would be ON TIME.

The station manager replied, "Madam, we are lucky if the train in ON THE TRACK."

Death Through Taxes

Both of these stories remind me of the very poor way the Church has dealt with the question of the Stewardship of Wealth in the last century. We are certainly *NOT*

ON TIME and I think it is because we haven't stayed on track. A great deal of the problems arose because many of the Lutherans that came to this country were from Europe, where the financing of the Church came mostly through State Taxes. The individual person never had a chance to grow in grace nor were they trained in the Grace of Giving, the kind of giving that is pleasing in God's sight.

Tracks Or Tragedy

To add to the tragedy, so many ministers have never been schooled to realize that Christian Stewardship is a "Work of God." It is not a purely human work. It is something that God works through believers and it involves Faith and even our faith is God's Gift to us through His church. St. Paul said it best when he stated, *"It is I, yet not I, Christ worketh in me."* Luther stressed it when he stated, "you are to become little Christ's to one another for the Lord's sake." This doesn't come easy. Nobody said it would. Jesus set the standard when he stated, *"Be perfect as the Father in Heaven is perfect."* You can see from this that this can never be the result of mere human endeavor. I'm sure God is aware of this fact and that is why He sent us His son, who is not only The Truth, and The Life, but also The Way. His very love convinces me that we are in this together and with such a partner I can never lose. He has a wonderful way of bringing me through His kind of victory. Thus it has become my daily prayer to seek His aid. That prayer I have titled "Letter Perfect."

Letter Perfect

Lord — Let me be steadfast in the midst of a stormy sea;
        Let me be loyal while others despise loyalty,

Lord — Let me be love when tempers burn fast into hate;
        Let me be patience when rashness stands close to my gate.

Lord — Let me be goodness, even when sin seems to pay;
        Let me be mercy when sin meets its terrible day.

Lord — Let me be trust when staggering facts all deny;
        Let me be hope in the face of a fog-blackened sky.

Lord — Let me be Thine even when I fail to be;
        Let me be new — a living copy of Thee.

                                    Amen.